TAKE CONTROL
OF YOUR
GAME

A LEARNING GUIDE
FOR SIMPLE and CONSISTENT
GOLF

TERRY MYERS

Take Control of Your Game

Author may be contacted at:

WOA Publications
Post Office Box 2448
Cupertino, Ca. 95015

Published by WOA Publications
ISBN 0-9679153-0-9
Library of Congress Card Number 00-190340

Illustrations by Crystal McCormick

A book on golf instruction

Checkout Terry's website at: www.terrymyers.com

Printed in the United States of America

ACKNOWLEDGEMENTS

To Renee Myers, my wife and best friend.

My parents, Don and Alice for their support.

Mike Paul, a great friend and fellow professional for all his help and support over the years.

Rich Brown, the instigator and motivator of this project.

Crystal McCormick, a wonderful illustrator.

Big Jon Bollum, Kellie Sutherland and Matt Cosbie at BR Printers for their generous help and patience.

Lee Martin, the first professional who inspired and helped me with my game.

Derek Hardy, the professional who taught me how to teach.

Dr. David Wright, the professional who took the time to help me learn.

The staffs of Saddle Creek Golf Club and Santa Clara Golf & Tennis Club, who have made and continue to make my job easier.

Mike Kim, the golf model.

To all my students who have made my job fun, I learn from you everyday.

INTRODUCTION

The reason for writing this book was to be able to direct my students to a written form of what I was teaching them and to see if I actually could put it down on paper.

My message is to teach students my knowledge of the game in a simplified form.

The students then must be able to take ownership of what they have learned.

I believe in what I call PROACTIVE teaching (building) rather than REACTIVE teaching (repairing).

In the early years of my teaching I tended to be a reactive teacher but found out I was more successful being a proactive teacher because my student's improvement was remarkably better.

I have spent a lot of time, traveled many pathways and destroyed some brain cells acquiring this knowledge.

Now I would like to share it with you.

ENJOY THE BOOK.

Terry Myers

Member of the Professional Golfers Association of America
Class 'A' Professional

TABLE OF CONTENTS

My advice would be to work on ONE piece of your game at a time paying attention to each step in the process. This will make it easier for you to develop and improve faster with less effort. This will save you time and money.

Sometimes you can look at something over and over again and then one day you look again and finally see something totally different or it has a new meaning or understanding. I find this to be one of the truly amazing things about life.

TABLE OF CONTENTS

Never be afraid to ask WHY or HOW. In my early years I was not popular with adults when I wanted to know the why and how of things. I was always being told to "Do as your told and be quiet". I wanted to learn and understand. For that I was labeled a bad attitude. Today things have changed. If someone is unwilling or unable to explain the why and how then find somebody else who will and can.

INTRODUCTION TO THE LONG GAME/SWING

SOME THINGS TO THINK ABOUT

The swing/long game is very important in that it gives the player the opportunity to get as close to the hole before turning to the short game to get the ball into the hole in the least amount of strokes.

Is there ONE way to swing a club successfully? NO.

Now I believe some swings are more successful.

Do all successful swings have certain fundamentals present? YES.

Do all swings have preferences used by each individual player? YES.

Is one preference better than another? NO.

It all depends on each individual, what he or she wants to do.

Nobody is the same we are all different.

JUST LOOK AT WHAT EVERYBODY IS WEARING AT THE GOLF COURSE and WHAT KIND OF CAR THEY DROVE TO GET THERE.

HOW MANY ARE WEARING THE SAME CLOTHES?
OR DRIVING THE SAME KIND OF CAR?

AND if they are the same are the colors different?

SET UP POSITIONS

THE FOUR BASICS

GRIP
STANCE
BALL POSITION
AIM & ALIGNMENT

Without proper set-up positions the swing will not be
CONSISTENT or EFFICIENT.

Practicing or playing without paying attention to these fundamentals is
hazardous to your game.

GOOD PLAYERS CONSTANTLY WORK ON THESE FUNDAMENTALS.

Should you?

SET UP POSITIONS

"The grip"

I am going to start first with how your hands
are going to work as a single unit before placing
them on the grip.

I recommend two choices of style of grip.

The first is called *interlocking*.
Preferred by players with smaller hands.

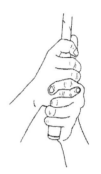

The second is called *overlapping*.
The most popular grip choice.

You may have to experiment with each grip to find out which one feels and works the best for you.

The choice is yours.

SET UP POSITIONS

"The grip"

To prevent hand damage and have better control of the club grip start with your left hand 1/2 inch below the top of the grip.

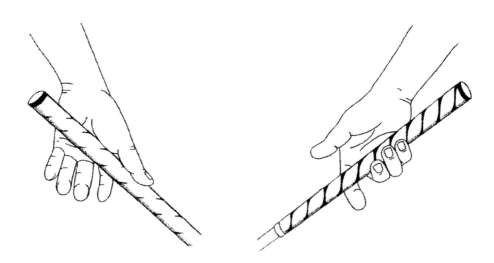

The grip with the left-hand will be positioned across your palm. The grip with the right hand will be positioned across the fingers.

SET UP POSITIONS

"The grip"

Some grip "definitions" for positioning of your hands. A "neutral" position you will be able to look down and see two knuckles on your left hand. A "neutral" position makes it easier to square the clubface during the swing.

If you see "three knuckles or more" then your grip is in a "strong" position. The tendency is for the clubface to "close" during the swing.

If you see "less than two knuckles" then your grip is in a "weak" position. The tendency is for the clubface to "open" during the swing.

SET UP POSITIONS

"The grip"

With the left hand grip in the two knuckle position and the right hand in the fingers the V's between the thumb and finger of both hands will point to the inside of the right underarm/shoulder. Check your positions in a mirror or window.

Both the "strong" and "weak" grip positions make it more difficult to control the clubface during the swing.

My recommendation is to have your grip in a "two knuckle" neutral position. It makes swinging the club a lot easier to learn.

REMEMBER: The "GRIP" is ALWAYS the PREFERENCE of the PLAYER.

Some great players have played from both "weak" and "strong" positions and been very successful. Experiment to find what works best for your game.

SET UP POSITIONS

"The grip"

The last part of the "grip" is the amount of pressure you will use to hold or grip the club. In the beginning the tendency will be to hold the club extremely firm because the club and swinging motions are uncomfortable to us.

As you become more comfortable with the club and swinging, the pressure should adjust to what I would best describe is the firmness in which you hold on to the steering wheel of your car while driving.

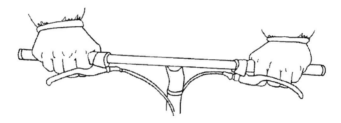

For juniors who do not drive, how about the pressure in which you hold on to the handlebars on your bike.

ONE LAST NOTE ON THE GRIP: If you want to make a grip change please do it in VERY SMALL increments rather than trying to change it all at once.

The only part attached to the club is your HANDS.

It will be easier this way and less traumatic to your swing.

SET UP POSITIONS

"The Stance"

The width of the stance is shoulder width. This will obviously be different with each player. Both feet will angle slightly outward about 20 degrees.

The legs will have a very slight bend at the knees.

SET UP POSITIONS

"The Stance"

To create the correct distance away from the ball take your club and rest it on the heel of the club then use a hand width of space from the top of the grip and the inside of your left thigh. The outside of the club (toe) will rise only 1/8 to 1/4 of an inch.

SET UP POSITIONS

"The Stance"

Any bending to get to the ball will be done with the waist/hip movement. You should feel the pressure there and not in your back.

This will form a relatively straight line with your back.

SET UP POSITIONS

"Ball Position"

I recommend having a ball position with all clubs forward of the center of your stance.

In all hitting or kicking sports the ball must be forward of center in order to effectively launch the ball.

Now this is a preference of the player. You may play the ball in any position you like.
Give it some thought and experiment with what works best for you.

SET UP POSITIONS

"Ball Position"

The ball is aligned in the center of the clubface. I know this sounds really obvious but I am constantly surprised where players line up the ball.

The club shaft is now in a straight line with ball position left of center and grip inside left thigh. This creates a CONSISTENT starting position for all your clubs.

REMEMBER THE BALL POSITION IS A PREFERENCE. So whatever positioning you decide, make sure that you do it the same way all the time in order to be as CONSISTENT as possible.

SET UP POSITIONS

"Aim and alignment"

Alignment of your body to a target is done through parallel lines to the target. You must first figure out your target line. The target line is from the ball to the target. You may use a club next to the ball to align the ball with the target.

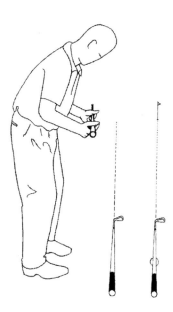

Now align the stance of your feet, hips and shoulders as close to parallel to the target line you have made with the club. Next put a club down that runs parallel to the target line to help you align your body.

SET UP POSITIONS

"Aim and alignment"

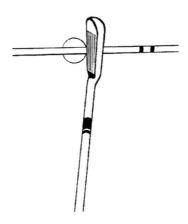

To align the clubface to the target you must create a 90-degree angle with the clubface's leading edge (bottom edge of club) to target line.

CLUBFACE ALIGNMENT IS SO IMPORTANT TO CREATING CONSISTENT SHOTS!

YOU MUST PAY ATTENTION TO IT AT ALL TIMES.

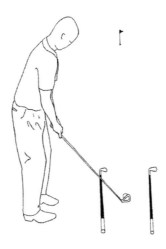

I RECOMMEND THAT YOU PRACTICE WITH CLUBS ON THE GROUND TO HELP GET THE "FEEL" OF PROPER ALIGNMENT.

SET UP POSITIONS

"Aim and alignment"

One way to make aiming and aligning easier is to do what is called "spot aiming". Picking a spot, something like a piece of grass or dirt that is in line with your target.

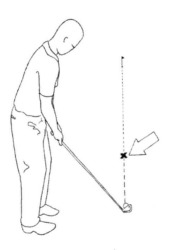

Once you have picked the spot, align your clubface and body to the spot.

SPOT AIMING IS USED BY A LOT OF GOOD PLAYERS TO HELP THEM WITH AIM & ALIGNMENT. GIVE IT A TRY, IT DOES WORK.

A PLACE TO WRITE YOUR NOTES
SET-UP POSITIONS

_____

_____

_____

_____

_____

_____

_____

_____

_____

_____

_____

_____

PLANE, PATH & ARC OF SWING

THE UNDERSTANDING

THE DEFINITIONS
A SIMPLE WAY TO CREATE

The golf swing must be on plane in order to have directional and trajectory control.

The golf swing must be on the proper pathway to have directional control.

The golf swing must have good arc width to create distance and accuracy.

Learning to swing the club on plane, good pathway and wide arc is very important in order to have a consistent swing.

Having something simple to do to swing on plane, good pathway and wide arc will make learning easier, development faster and create consistency under stress.

PLANE, PATH & ARC OF SWING

"The definitions"

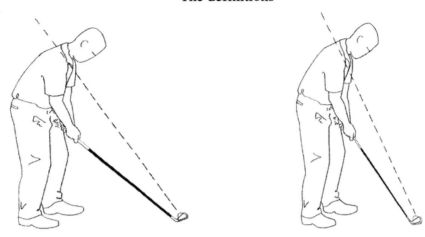

The *plane* of the swing is the angle in which the club is swung. Everybody has a natural swing plane. The angle is measured from the ball to the top of the shoulder and up.

The plane angle will be different with each club. The longer the club the flatter the angle as illustrated on the left and the shorter the club the steeper the angle will be as illustrated on the right.

But the swing will be the same with each club; it will just appear different.

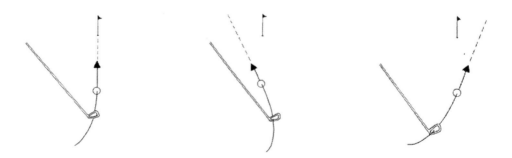

The *path* of the swing is the direction in which the club is swung, such as straight, to the right or left of the target.

PLANE, PATH & ARC OF SWING

"The definitions"

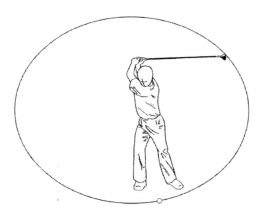

The *arc* of the swing is the width in which the club is swung. Longer clubs will be able to generate a wider arc.

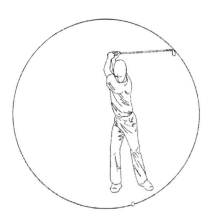

The shorter clubs will generate a smaller arc.

PLANE, PATH and ARC OF SWING

"The understanding of plane"

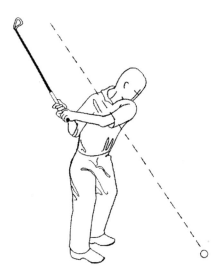

The swing plane is a circular motion that works best when on your natural plane angle.

If the swing is too low (flat level) it will not work as consistently as a swing on your natural plane angle.

If the swing is too high (upright) it will not work as consistently as a swing on your natural plane angle.

PLANE, PATH and ARC OF SWING

"The understanding of plane"

The swing on the natural plane angle.

You can still swing and strike a golf ball from any plane angle.

The angle in which you swing is your CHOICE.

I believe that the swing works more CONSISTENTLY on the plane angle that is determined by your body.

PLANE, PATH & ARC OF SWING

"The understanding of path"

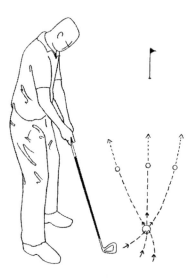

The path of the swing will propel the ball either STRAIGHT, RIGHT or LEFT.

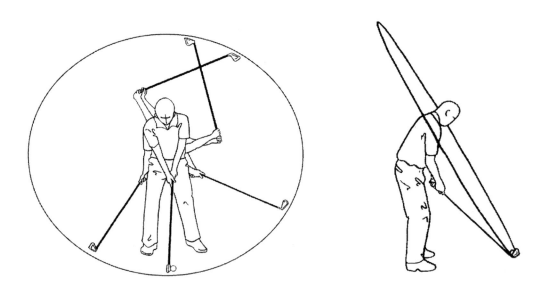

The path of the swing works in a circular motion. The swing does not work on a line that is flat on the ground. A swing is like a wheel working in a round form. There are NO FLAT spots on a wheel.

PLANE, PATH and ARC OF SWING

"The understanding of arc"

The arc of the swing is also a circular motion and creates force. A larger or wider arc will create more force than a smaller arc. The goal would be to create your widest arc possible.

A GOOD SWING IS ONE THAT IS ON PLANE, ON THE CORRECT PATHWAY AND HAS THE WIDEST ARC.

NOW ALL THREE OF THESE PIECES CAN WORK FOR OR AGAINST EACH OTHER.

"Things to think about"

IF THE SWING IS NOT ON PLANE,

NOT ON THE CORRECT PATHWAY,

OR THE WIDEST ARC

Then MANIPULATIONS and COMPENSATIONS must be made in order TO GET THE BALL to go where you WANT IT TO GO.

If you can!

THAT MAKES GOLF HARDER!

PLANE, PATH & ARC OF SWING

"A simple way to create your natural plane, correct path and the widest arc"

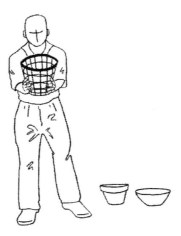

To start you will need a range ball basket or something that resembles it such as a bowl or pot without the plant.

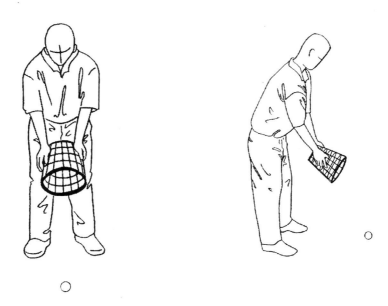

Now get into your set up position of stance with the basket. Hands will be positioned as if you have a club in set up position.

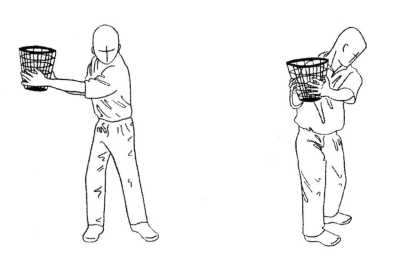

Next turn your shoulders 90-degrees and your hips 45-degrees to the right and raise the basket to position #1. Now if the basket had water in it you would not want the water to spill out. The reference points would be if you stuck both arms out to your sides thus creating a 180-degree half circle. Make sure your arms are extended to create some width.

Now keeping moving your arms to position #2 so if the basket had water in it the water would spill onto the middle of your right shoulder. (Plane, path and arc)

PLANE. PATH & ARC OF SWING

Next turn the basket to the left to position #3. This is exactly the mirror image of position #1 except that your legs and feet begin a transfer to the finish position. Again the reference point is the basket travels in a 180-degree half circle.

Now raise your arms to position #4 so that if the basket had water in it the water would spill onto the middle of your left shoulder.

This simple basket swing creates a swing that is on your optimal plane, the correct swing path and the widest arc.

PLANE, PATH & ARC OF SWING

"The basket applied to the club"
Front view

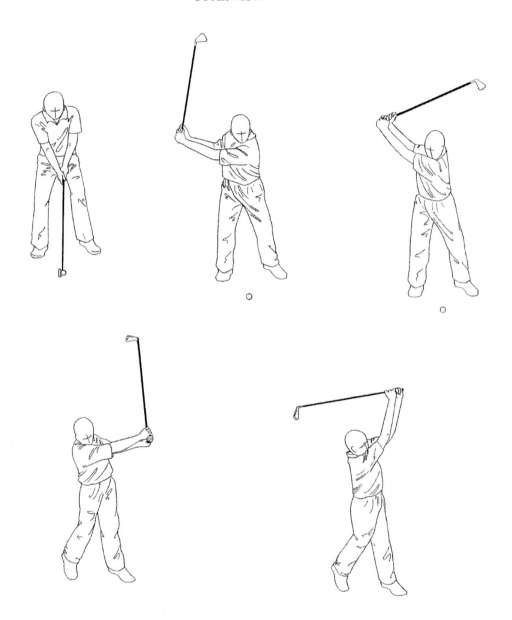

Now that you have done your basket exercise/drill, apply it to your swing with the club.

PLANE, PATH & ARC OF SWING

"The basket applied to the club"
Side view

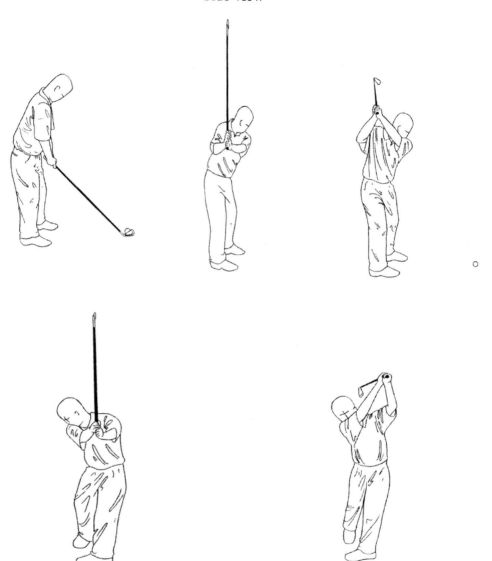

The basket is much easier to do than with the club, it becomes easier to do as you practice more repetitions.

HOW MANY REPETITIONS TO BECOME EFFICIENT?

This drill creates your natural plane, the correct swing path and the widest arc all in one without having to think about anything except swinging the basket.

During my years of teaching I have never seen anything that works likes this to create so much without trying to remember 30 things while you swing. If you work with this exercise/drill you will be amazed at what you can accomplish. I have seen too many students who shot in the 100's who now play at a single digit handicap.

Remember it is not how much you practice (quantity) but what you practice (quality).

You can really improve with large quantities of quality practice!

A PLACE TO WRITE YOUR NOTES
PLANE, PATH and ARC.

SEVEN DIMENSIONS
OF CONTACT

SPINE ANGLE & SWING CENTER

TOPPED, FAT, THIN, OFF THE HOSEL AND TOE

I believe that this is the most important element of the golf swing and short game.

Learning to make better contact with the ball, creating solid shots is essential to playing CONSISTENT golf.

You could have a great looking swing but without good contact it will be unproductive at best and vice versa have a bad looking swing with good contact and be really productive.

KEEPING YOUR HEAD DOWN AND EYE ON THE BALL *IS NOT* GOING TO GET THE JOB DONE! "Old school" stuff.

SEVEN DIMENSIONS OF CONTACT

To create solid contact with the 'sweet spot' on the club during the swing you must first know how it works.

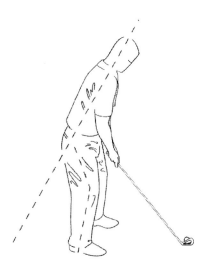

First get into your set up position to address the ball.
Now you have created your *spine/body angle*. The legs are also in an angle.

Next we will locate our *swing center.* This is the center of our body as illustrated by the dotted line when addressing the ball.

SEVEN DIMENSIONS OF CONTACT

"The understanding of centrifugal force factors"

While attempting to make a swing at the ball your arms, hands and club will straighten out at impact with your left first then the right through the centrifugal force.

That will create a constant variable to work with.

This will not apply to pitch and chip shots due to the lack of force.

THE HEAD & EYES

If you were told to keep your head down and eyes on the ball to produce good contact then you were misled. Try this experiment.

Stand at address position and rotate your head. Does your body move?   NO.
NEXT close your eyes and rotate your head. Does your body move?   NO.

If you know your arms straighten out at impact through the centrifugal force and if your spine/body angle stays in the original address position then you will achieve good contact with the ball.
Does it make a difference what your head and eyes have done?
Check out David Duval and Anika Sorenstam on the professional tours.

Most of us feel more comfortable looking at the ball while swinging to make sure the ball is still there. It's a good idea. You wouldn't want to panic about "where is the ball"?

SEVEN DIMENSIONS OF CONTACT

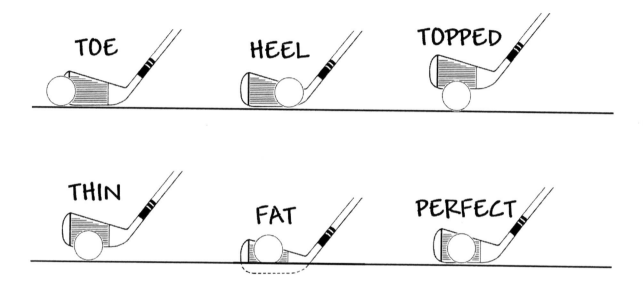

Identification and definitions of shot patterns on the clubface.

SEVEN DIMENSIONS OF CONTACT

The favorite undesirable contact is the topped, thin or complete 'airball'.
The spine angle has *raised* out of the original position. Could the angle of your legs have changed the angle of your body? YES. This will apply to the next examples.

The second undesirable contact is the fat or striking the turf before ball.
The spine angle has *lowered* down from the original position.

The third undesirable contact is the toe or outside of the center.
The spine angle has *pulled away* from the original position.

The fourth undesirable contact is the shank or inside of center.
The spine angle has *moved across* from the original position.

SEVEN DIMENSIONS OF CONTACT

The fifth undesirable contact is the fat or behind the ball 'drop kick'.
The spine angle has *tilted back and down* from the original position.

The sixth undesirable contact is thin or too high of contact on the ball.
The swing center has moved *laterally back* and stayed there from the original position.

SEVEN DIMENSIONS OF CONTACT

The last undesirable contact is also thin or too high of contact on the ball.
The swing center has moved laterally *forward* and stayed there from the original position.

LEARNING TO IMPROVE

In order to create a consistent "solid" contact with the "sweet spot" on the club the player must learn from the physical evidence left by the ball mark on the club or the vibrations he or she feels through the grip during contact with the ball.

REMEMBER THE BALL DOES NOT LIE, ALWAYS TRUST PHYSICAL EVIDENCE!

How do you learn?

By applying the "feedback" to the next swing.

For example if you topped the last shot you know that your spine angle has raised out of its original position and on the next swing you would try to maintain your spine angle and not raise it out of position.

SEVEN DIMENSIONS OF CONTACT

In order to adjust the next swing you must "feel" the body/spine angle move out of position.

If you can not "feel" the movement then all you can do is try to "copy or mimic" the desired adjustment.

Someday you will "feel" the movement and when that happens you will be able to make better adjustments. When will that happen?

Remember that everybody is different and each player will learn at different rates of time. The better hand/eye coordination you have the less time it will take to "feel" the movements.

Does it mean that if you do not have good hand/eye coordination that you will never "feel" the movements? NO, it will just take longer (more repetitions) but you will eventually "feel" the movements.

IT MAY TAKE LONGER THAN YOU THINK BUT HAVE SOME PATIENCE WITH YOURSELF.

SOME VALUABLE INFORMATION

Why do divots occur?

Divots (removal of turf by the club) are created by the down force of the golf club in relationship with the plane angle. A proper divot will start after the ball is struck and be a thin layer of turf.

If there is excessive turf being excavated after the ball is struck then the spine/ body angle has moved down after impact.

SEVEN DIMENSIONS OF CONTACT

So with a shorter club like a 9 iron you will have a tendency to take a divot since the plane angle is more upright than with a long iron or wooden/metal club.

With a longer club like a 3 iron you will have a tendency to not take a divot since the plane angle is flatter than with a short iron/club.

"SUCCESS"

YOU *CAN* DO ANYTHING YOU SET YOUR MIND TO DO!

The use of the word I CAN'T always reinforces your mind and body that you are unable to SUCCEED.

The use of the word I CAN allows you to SUCCEED.

SEVEN DIMENSIONS OF CONTACT

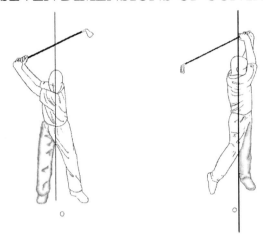

The one misconception I have seen done by a lot of players is the *weight transfer* from the right side lower body to the left side during the swing. It should happen in all swings with the *swing center* maintaining its original position.

I believe the *swing center* must not move laterally back or forward with the *weight transfer.* Why sacrifice your ability to make good solid contact and directional control of your shot?

You could time the lateral shifting perfectly to put it back to the same place as you started but you will probably be very inconsistent at best or you would have to practice more than someone who did not.
REMEMBER it is your choice.

SWING WHERE YOU CAN SEE YOUR SHADOW OR IN A MIRROR/ WINDOW TO CHECK THE LATERAL MOVEMENT.

Check this out in the DRILLS & AIDS Chapter.

A PLACE FOR YOUR NOTES
7 DIMENSIONS of CONTACT

CURVATURE OF THE BALL

THE 9 BALL FLIGHT LAWS

STRAIGHT, HOOK/DRAW and SLICE/FADE

"A reality of the game"

IF YOU CAN NOT CONTROL THE CURVE OF YOUR SHOT,
THE GAME OF GOLF WILL BE FRUSTRATING AT BEST AND
YOUR GAME WILL NOT BE CONSISTENT.

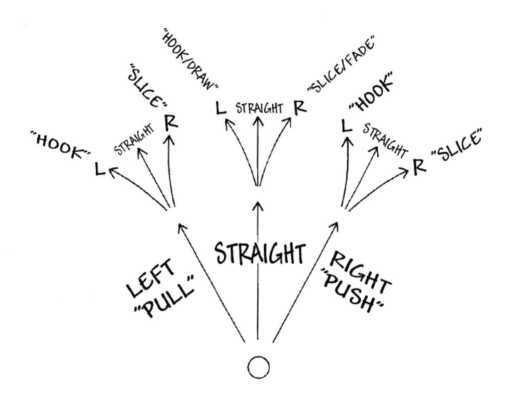

THE 9 BALL FLIGHT LAWS

The swing plane/pathway starts the ball on its initial direction either STRAIGHT, RIGHT OR LEFT.

Then the ball goes either STRAIGHT, RIGHT OR LEFT thus creating the "9" different ball flight laws.

CURVATURE OF THE BALL

To understand ball flight laws you will divide the flight of the ball into *TWO* separate halves.

The PATHWAY of the swing will send the ball off on the *FIRST* half of flight.

The CLUBFACE ANGLE at impact with the ball creates the ball flight on the *SECOND* half of the flight.

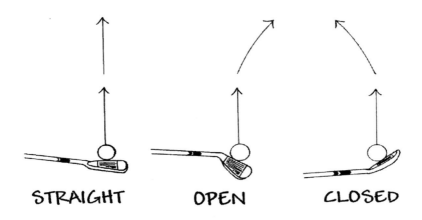

For example if our plane/pathway sends the ball initially straight and then the ball goes STRAIGHT the clubface is SQUARE at impact as illustrated on the left.

If the pathway is straight and the clubface is OPEN then ball will curve right on the second half of flight as illustrated in the center.

If the pathway is straight and the clubface is CLOSED the ball will curve to the left as illustrated on the right.

CURVATURE OF THE BALL

"How do I try to control the clubface angle so my shots go where I want"?

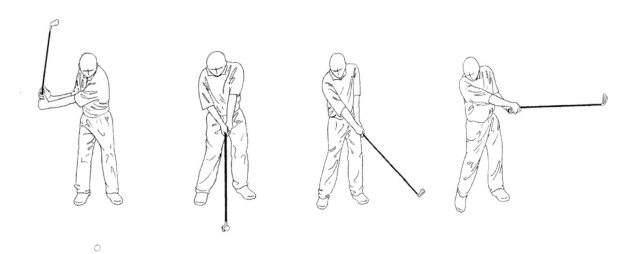

To get the desired clubface position at impact you must "release the club".

To release the club you must first learn to rotate your forearms/wrist/hand.

CURVATURE OF THE BALL

The second thing is developing a 'feeling' for the TIMING (WHEN DO I DO THIS) of the rotation of the forearms/wrist/hand.

The easiest way to do this is to watch the curvature of your shot pattern (Straight, right or left) and adjust the timing according the result.

How do I adjust?

If you feel the rotation of the forearms but your ball is still turning to the right the timing of the rotation is what I call "late" making the clubface "open" at impact.

This is called a 'slice' or fade (small movement to the right) when done on purpose.

To correct the curve the rotation of the forearms must be done "earlier" on the downswing.

You will have to make an adjustment to what you "feel".

THE BALL WILL ALWAYS TELL YOU THE "TRUTH".

ALWAYS TRUST WHAT THE BALL IS DOING FOR THE "CORRECT" FEEDBACK.

ADJUST TO WHAT THE BALL IS TELLING YOU AND NOT WHAT YOUR ARMS/BODY ARE TELLING YOU.

CURVATURE OF THE BALL

"How do I adjust?"

Now if you feel the rotation of the forearms and the ball is curving to the left the timing of the rotation is what I call "early" making the clubface "closed" at impact.

This is called a 'hook' or draw (small movement to the left) when done on purpose.

To correct the curve the rotation must be 'delayed' on the downswing.

You will have to make an adjustment to what you "feel"

Everybody will "feel" this rotation of the forearms for the desired curvature of the ball DIFFERENTLY.

ALWAYS TRUST THE FLIGHT OF THE BALL TO TEACH YOU WHAT YOU NEED TO FEEL TO CREATE THE DESIRED PATTERN.

REMEMBER THE BALL NEVER LIES BUT OUR ARMS/BODY CAN AND DOES.

You will have to continually work on this timing forever if you want to have control of your shot pattern.

This is a lifetime fundamental.

This is not a "natural" movement for almost everybody who has learned how to play the game; there have been a few rare exceptions.

"Some other factors that influence the curvature of the ball"

For example if you move the swing center back laterally your forearm/wrist/hand will be further away from the impact area usually resulting in a "early" rotation thus closing the clubface but could also create no rotation thus resulting in a open clubface.

CURVATURE OF THE BALL

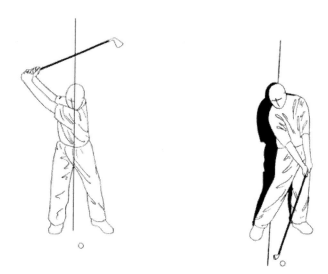

The opposite will happen if you move forward laterally the forearm/wrist/hand will be closer to the impact area usually resulting in a "late" rotation resulting in an open clubface.

If you use your right shoulder to "release the club" you will have the tendency to pull the ball to the left on the initial flight.
This sometimes works with the shorter clubs but with the longer clubs the clubface will be 'open' thus producing a 'slicing' curvature pattern to the right.

CURVATURE OF THE BALL

Now I will touch the idea of presetting the clubface closed or open to achieve the desired shot pattern or cure your problems.

This will not work unless you have FOREARM rotation to "release the club" in your swing.

Check out all the anti-slice clubs on the market with built in closed clubface angle. I have seen many slices from players with that type of equipment.

You can not buy a good golf game!

PUTTING DUCT TAPE OR BAND-AIDS ON IT WILL NOT CURE YOUR PROBLEMS.

YOU MUST PAY YOUR DUES through practice and learning from your practice!

IS THIS GOING TO BE EASY?   OF COURSE NOT!

Can you do this? YES you CAN! If I can learn it so can you.

CURVATURE OF THE BALL

"Advanced Ideas"

Good players have practiced "releasing the club" for a long time thus building up a good "feeling" for the timing.

This gives the player control of his/her shot.

That creates "confidence" in knowing where the ball will go.

Depending upon their preference some good players will play a "draw" or "fade" shot pattern almost exclusively by timing the rotation so the clubface is a little closed for the draw or a little open for the fade.

Over my many years of observation of good players to poor players I have come to some conclusions.

All good players have a forearm/wrist/hand rotation that creates the release of their club thus generating control of their shot pattern.

All poor players either have very poor forearm rotation or none at all (the later being the most likely) thus generating a loss of control of the shot pattern (slicing and hooking).

This makes the game too hard to play if you are missing or do not understand this fundamental.

A SAFE PLACE TO WRITE YOUR NOTES
CURVATURE OF THE BALL

ADVANCED SECTION

ARE YOU READY FOR MORE?

DOWNSWING SEQUENCE
TEMPO & RHYTHM

The last few pieces to tie in to your swing once you feel ready and have some control over the other four fundamentals; set-up positions, plane/pathway/arc, contact between club/ball and curvature/clubface angle.

Understanding these next pieces will make the other fundamental elements easier to work with and perform.

Learning to swing and play this game is a PROCESS that should be done on a step by step basis.

"Downswing sequence"

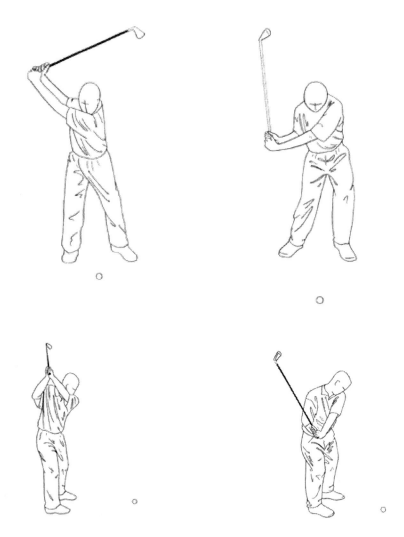

"A very important process"

The downswing starts with the hips, which have turned to 45 degrees in the backswing. The hips turn back to the original position of address.

This motion will pull the club, hands, arms and shoulders into the correct position for proper PATHWAY and to be able to "release the club".

"Downswing sequence"

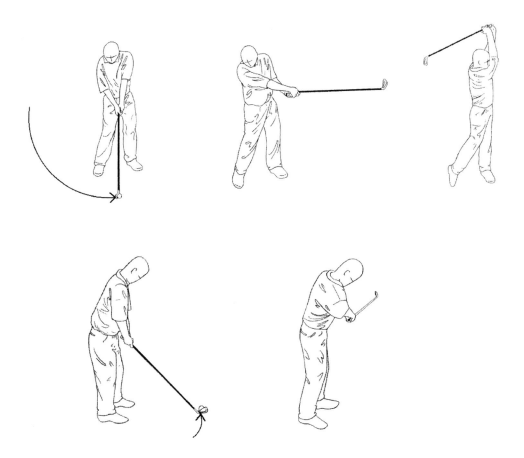

Next the hands, arms and shoulder/upper body swings the club through and you will also be "releasing the club with the forearm rotation".

THE BIG KEY: The RIGHT elbow must pass the outer RIGHT hipbone before the hips can resume moving from the square position to a finish position. This will also create a firm left side to swing against thus creating a push/pull effect for more power.

THIS HAPPENS SO FAST, IN JUST A FRACTION OF A SECOND.

ADVANCED SECTION

"Why do we do this?"

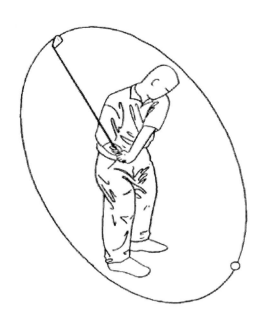

MORE POWER AND ENERGY

This will allow the club to properly swing on the correct plane/pathway and give you the opportunity to retain an angle between the shaft and arms.

This angle produces an enormous amount of energy.

This is called "lag".

The smaller the angle between the forearm and the club-shaft the more energy will be released into the ball thus creating POWER.

This takes a lot of practice to create a smaller angle.

"What if?"

If this sequence does not happen in the right order and the hips move before the right elbow passes through, trouble will arise if you want your ball to start out STRAIGHT.

You will start the PATHWAY of the swing either RIGHT (push) or LEFT (pull) because the hip is BLOCKING the space in which you want to swing in.

The club will have no choice but to swing around the hip.

The club is traveling too FAST for you to be able to change it. Try grabbing on to something moving at over 50 miles per hour. GOOD LUCK.

That is the law of MOTION (physics) at work.

"Power loss"

LOST ANGLE
CASTING

Again if the sequence does not happen and you start the swing incorrectly the angle is lost.

The greater the angle between the forearms and the club-shaft the greater the power loss.

This is called "casting the club".

ALL ACTIVITIES INVOLVING A SWING TO STRIKE AN OBJECT
REQUIRE THE RETENTION OF THIS ANGLE.

HAMMERING NAILS
TENNIS
BASEBALL
ANY KICKING SPORT

JUST THINK ABOUT IT FOR A SECOND.

"Tempo & Rhythm"

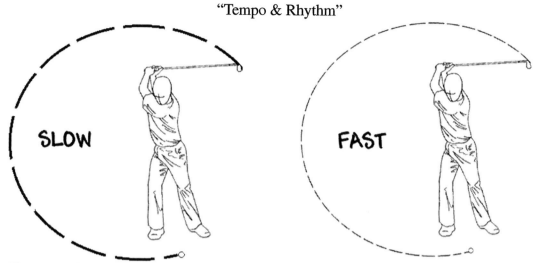

To create the perfect "tempo and rhythm" to your swing you must first figure out your "rhythm". It will depend on your personality or pace in which you do things in life.

Now that may be a little slower or faster than other player's but that is OK because we are all different.

Once you have established your comfortable pace of swing you will need to know how to use it most efficiently with "tempo".

To understand the way "tempo" works think of it in terms of gears like your car transmission. You have 1st through 4th gears. "Tempo" is swinging the club in the same gear all the way through the entire swing.

"Tempo & Rhythm"

Trouble will exist if you try to go from say 1st gear to 4th gear to hit the ball farther. Major male player problem. I wonder why?

To better understand "why?" this does not work think of how a 'sling shot' works when you pull back the rubber band.

Is there a lot of energy stored up?

Now do you let go of the rubber band or do you try to push it faster with your hand?

"Tempo & Rhythm"

The golf swing works the same way with the body coiling and turning 90 degrees against two fixed points (your legs and feet) creating a lot of stored up energy waiting to be released.

The problem is that we are unable to "feel" the stored up energy so we try to "add" some not realizing that is unnecessary for more power.

All you really have to do is let go and the swing will go very fast on its own.

IF THE SWING IS NOT DONE IN THE RIGHT TEMPO a lot of bad effects will BEGIN to arise.

ANOTHER PLACE FOR YOUR NOTES
ADVANCED SECTION

DRILLS & AIDS DEPARTMENT

THE KEY TO SUCCESSFUL FUNDAMENTALS

When I was first learning to play this game I hated to do the drills given by the Professional.

I thought it was more fun to wail away at the ball with my driver.

Soon reality set in and my scores did not improve to my liking and wailing away at my driver was not going to make my scores lower.

An amazing thing happened to my game once I started to do the drills.

They are the reason why I am able to play this game on a professional skill level.

The reality is that drills are not the most fun things to do but will produce the biggest reward in your game.

MY MESSAGE IS SIMPLE: DO THE DRILLS IF YOU WANT TO PLAY BETTER.

This drill is by far the best thing I have ever seen to develop a great golf swing.

Once again not only will the drill create your natural plane, pathway and arc of swing but will automatically reinforce the proper downswing sequence.

HAVE SOME PATIENCE before giving up on something that may not work instantly.

If you do this 3 days a week for 15 minutes each day over a PERIOD OF TIME it will surprise you.

My definition of a PERIOD OF TIME is 3 to 6 months.

I would advise you to continue doing the drill the rest of your golf career.

THE DRILL will provide CONSISTENCY in your swing.

DRILLS & AIDS DEPARTMENT

"Swinging with your feet together drill"

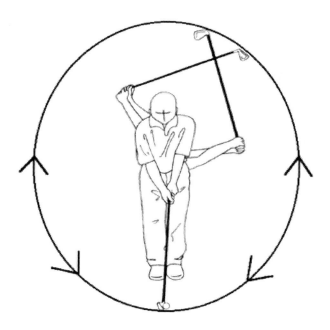

This drill has been around for longer than most of us have been alive and it works unbelievably well in developing your: SPINE/BODY ANGLE, THE DOWN SWING SEQUENCE, BALANCE (for better spine/body angle) and TEMPO & RHYTHM.

To do this drill put both of your feet together and address the ball the same as you would in you normal swing.

The ball position will be on the inside of the left heel.

NOW JUST SWING the club as you would in your normal swing motion.

This may feel awkward at first but will get easier and more comfortable as you do more repetitions.

My students success with this drill scares me because it works so well. Try it out. It works!

DRILLS & AIDS DEPARTMENT

"Rapid fire ball drill"

This drill has also been around for a long time and really works very well.

It will develop your ability to swing the club in what I would describe a "free swing".

What do I mean by "free swing"?

A SWING WITHOUT MUSCLE TENSION

Tight or restricted muscles do not work as well as relaxed ones.

Muscle tension comes from your mind/brain messages.

Messages that you want to control the swing or club.

This will reduce your ability to create DISTANCE and DIRECTION.

If you are on an artificial grass mat line up 4-5 balls in a row about 3 inches apart.

If you are on grass line up 10 balls in a row about 3 inches apart.

"Rapid fire ball drill" (continued)

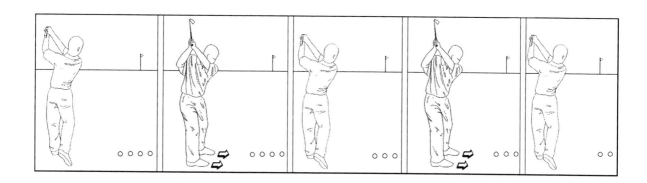

Next address the first ball and swing normally, then from your finish position swing the club back to the top of your back swing and then step forward 3 inches and swing at the second ball then repeat the same for the next balls in the row.

The motion should be done with NO STOPPING at all between the swings.

If there is then you are not "free swinging" because you thought about it during the drill.

LEARN TO NOT CARE WHERE THE BALL GOES.

THE MORE YOU CARE THE WORSE YOUR SWING GETS.

EVER WONDER WHY YOUR PRACTICE SWING IS SO GOOD and YOUR SWING WITH THE BALL IS DIFFERENT?

The drill frees up your mind so your body can work in a relaxed state.

It works because you do not have time to think.

DRILLS & AIDS DEPARTMENT

To create really good contact with ball you must train your body to be more stable with your spine/body angle.
The next three drills create the FEEL your body needs for more CONSISTENT contact between the club and ball.

"Swing in a shadow drill"

Mark a spot on the ground and line up your swing center with the spot.

Now swing your club to the top of the backswing and look at your shadow to see if it has moved from the original position of your swing center and spine/body angle as you were at address.

Next swing to your finish position and look to see if you are in the same place with your swing center and angle as you were at address.

You will be trying to keep the shadow of your swing center and spine angle from moving out of their original starting positions.

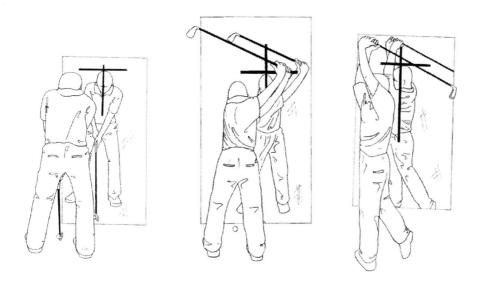

"Swing in a window or mirror drill"

This drill is very similar to the last drill except you can now view yourself to SEE the angle from a different perspective.

Place a long piece of tape on the window or mirror in a straight line or angle.

Repeat the swing process from the SHADOW drill to see if you can keep you swing center and spine/body angle from changing their original angles and positions.

Both of these two drills are very good because you can SEE any extra movement and be able to MAKE adjustments with your body and hopefully FEEL where the correct positions and angles should be.

REMEMBER: it takes time and patience to become CONSISTENT.

"The turn drill"

Take the club in your hands about shoulder width with your arms extending straight down as illustrated on the far left.

Now bend your elbows so that the club shaft almost touches your chest.

Next bend from your waist as you would to address the ball.

Then turn your torso back and forth keeping the club shaft at a slight angle.

You can also do this in a window or mirror to see if you can maintain your spine/body angle and swing center.

This drill is very good for all players to train their body to learn the FEEL for the proper BODY/SPINE angle while swinging the club.

DRILLS & AIDS DEPARTMENT

"CHIPPING & PITCHING DRILL"

"The throw"
(As demonstrated in the Chipping & Pitching Chapter)

A great teaching professional taught this drill to me when I was just learning the value of the short game.

In the beginning I was skeptical about how I was going to look to the other players but if the drill was going to work I did not care what the other players thought about what I was doing.

As I got older and became a better player I realized that this drill worked so well that I continue to use it twenty plus years later.

I also found out a lot of touring professionals learned the same drill I did and still continue to use the drill just as I do.

YES! I still throw balls because it works.

"PUTTING DRILL"

"Putting with the stripe"
(As demonstrated in the Putting Chapter)

This drill was given to me when I was about to give up the game because of my INCONSISTENT putting performance as a professional.

The guys who let me in on this back in the late 1980's actually felt sorry for me and decided that since my ball striking had also deteriorated because of my poor putting that I was no longer a threat to beat them anymore.

I thank them everyday for letting me know how a ball really rolls STRAIGHT.

I personally have seen some amazing things by using this drill.

BLOCK vs. RANDOM

"Different ways to practice"

BLOCK practice is taking one club and hitting balls continuously with that club.

This kind of practice should be done when working on the FUNDAMENTALS.

HIGHER HANDICAP PLAYERS DO THIS TYPE ONLY.

HOW DO YOU PRACTICE?

RANDOM practice is using one club at a time and rotating them on every swing.

Do you ever wonder why you can do so well on the range and not perform as well on the course?

This kind of practice should be done when preparing to go to the course.

You can even pretend to play a round of golf on a great course doing this.

Could this include just putting with ONE ball?

How about chipping or pitching with ONE ball?

POOR PLAYERS SELDOM USE THIS TYPE OF PRACTICE.

BETTER PLAYERS TEND TO USE this type PRACTICE more often.

DRILLS & AIDS DEPARTMENT

"Playing with the same type of ball"

I see this all the time from amateurs that I play with in pro-amateur events or with students and friends.

REMEMBER: All balls are not the same.

You should play with the same kind of ball all the time because of the CONSISTENCY factor.

Different balls go different distances based upon hardness and spin rates.

They also feel and react differently in the short game (chipping, pitching, bunker play and putting).

So find a ball you like to play with and stick with it for a while.

For example if you like the 'Flitleist' use nothing but that brand and make of ball.

SO EVEN IF YOU HUNT THE *"USED BALL BARREL"* BUY THE EXACT SAME BRAND AND MAKE. The numbers are for identification purposes only and mean nothing to the performance of the ball.

A PLACE TO SCRIBBLE NOTES
DRILLS & AIDS

_____

_____

_____

_____

_____

_____

_____

_____

_____

_____

_____

_____

INTRODUCTION TO THE SHORT GAME

HOW IMPORTANT IS THE SHORT GAME IN GOLF?

I started out as a player who shot in the 120's then became a scratch handicap player (handicap in the range of zero) in relatively short period of time, less than 18 months.

How did I improve so quickly?

Are you ready for my short game sermon? If so read on.

First of all let me define the short game as any shot played from 50 yards or closer to the hole.

I learned the value of the short game and how much time I should devote to that part of the game.

Of course I practiced more than the average player did but I learned what to practice to improve my scores.

Now most of the players I see today and of the past 20 plus years work exclusively on their long game and neglect or don't practice the short game at all and then expect to go out and shoot better scores.

When I started playing a PGA Professional told me that if I wanted to really improve my scores I would have to spend 2 hours on the short game for every hour spent on the long game.

I cheated a bit and spent 4 hours on the short game to every hour on the long game.

THE IMPROVEMENT I SAW WAS UNBELIEVABLE.

INTRODUCTION TO THE SHORT GAME

Some studies have been made of practice time ratios for the amateur and the professional/scratch golfers.

I found the results to be very truthful and was not shocked by them.

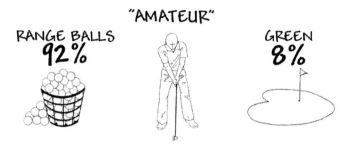

Amateur players only spend about 8% of their practice time on the short game and 92% on the long game.

The professional/scratch players spend 68% of their time on the short game and 32% on the long game.

Since I already knew this a long time ago I understood the studies.

The other part of the studies shows the average golf score has NOT CHANGED in over 25 years.

Now I know the conditions of maintenance has improved, the instruction has improved and the equipment has also improved yet the scores do not.

I think you can figure it out.

End of sermon.

CHIPPING

THE LOW RUNNING SHOT

THE THROW
THE STRATEGY

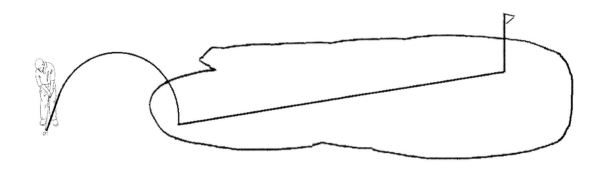

This is the beginning of learning how to improve your scores.

I believe the chip shot is the easiest of the short game skills.

That does not mean that this is easy.

I feel that this shot is more crucial as the player becomes a better ball striker.

FOR A PLAYER LOOKING TO IMPROVE THEIR SCORES THIS IS THE
ELEMENT TO START PRACTICING MORE.

In my mind you can NEVER practice too
much chipping.

CHIPPING

"The art of the low running shot to the green"

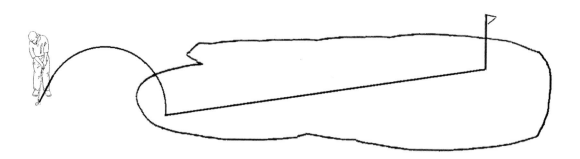

The chipping motion is used when the player chooses to play a low running shot to the green.

Club of choice for the shot ranges from the 4 iron to the sand wedge.

Is one club better than another? NO.

I think each individual will have to experiment with different club choices.

The choices will be based upon your distance from the hole.

Is it a short, medium or long shot?

Is it an uphill or downhill shot?

The lie of your ball in the grass.

Is it sitting up or down in the grass?

The speed/firmness of the green.

Are the greens fast or slow or wet or dry?

CHIPPING

"The strategy"

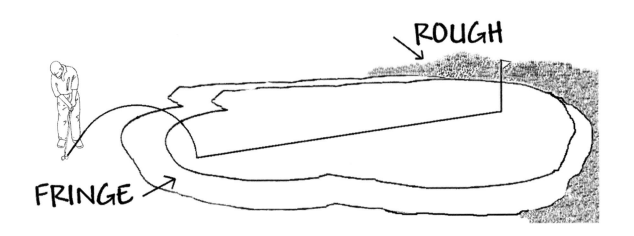

I believe the STRATEGY should be to get the ball onto the controlled surface (putting green) as soon as possible and roll the rest of the way to the hole.

Some strategies believe in flying the ball 1/3 of the way to the hole and roll 2/3rds.

I think that having to fly the ball the shortest distance is easier for the player because you will be doing less work.

Now this may require that you chip the ball with different clubs.

Experiment on your own to find what works best for you.

REMEMBER IT IS ALWAYS YOUR CHOICE on HOW TO PLAY EACH SHOT as long as you achieve your objective.

"GETTING THE BALL INTO THE HOLE IN THE LEAST AMOUNT OF STROKES"

CHIPPING

"The throw"

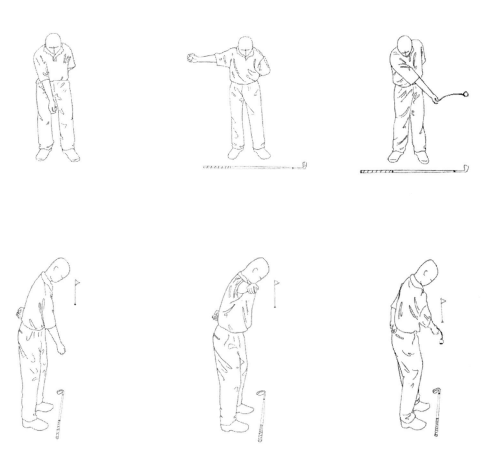

The best method I have found is what I call "the throwing of the ball".

First take the ball in your right hand and align your feet/body parallel to the hole/target.

Next swing your arm back in a straight line with the target and throw the ball with your arm swinging at the target to a LOW FINISH position with your hand facing the target.

CHIPPING

"The club is an extension of the arm"

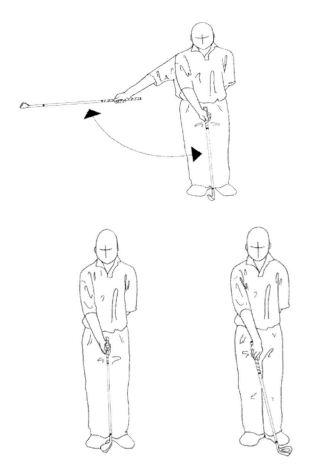

Now put the club you have chosen to chip with in your right hand.

Here's where you will have to use your imagination.

The grip and shaft of the club become an extension of your arm.

If you swing your arm back and forward the club follows.

The clubface will now become an extension of your hand.

If you turn your hand the clubface will turn.

CHIPPING

"Set up for the shot"

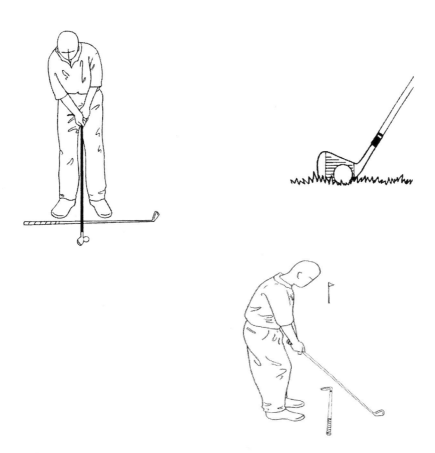

Now address the ball with your feet in a narrower stance and the ball position off the inside of the left heel to start with.

The club will be resting behind the ball and down in the grass with the ball in the center of the clubface.

You may choose after some practice and experimentation to alter the ball position.

That's OK and will be your preference.

CHIPPING

"Applying the throw with the club"

THE MOST IMPORTANT PART NOW IS TO USE YOUR RIGHT ARM AND
HAND TO CONTROL THE CLUB AND YOUR left arm and hand FOR
STABILITY ONLY.

Now execute the throw with the club with the ball in the way.

The club will travel in a straight line at the target and the leading edge of the clubface will
also be facing the target.

GO back to the strategy page in this chapter to figure out what you want to do.

A PLACE TO WRITE NOTES
CHIPPING

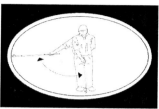

_____

_____

_____

_____

_____

_____

_____

_____

_____

_____

_____

_____

_____

PITCHING

THE HIGH FLYING SHOT

THE STRATEGY
THE THROW

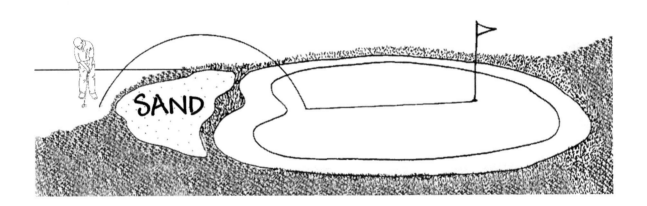

The pitching shot is quite a bit more difficult than chipping.

I would recommend that you become proficient at chipping before adding pitching to your repertoire of shot making skills.

As you learn to play on the course, especially for beginners, you will find that this shot will be a big factor in determining the score you will shoot each round.

That is because you will have a lot of them.

If you want more from your game, this is a necessary shot to learn in further developing your ability to shoot lower scores.

PITCHING

"The art of the high flying shot to the green"

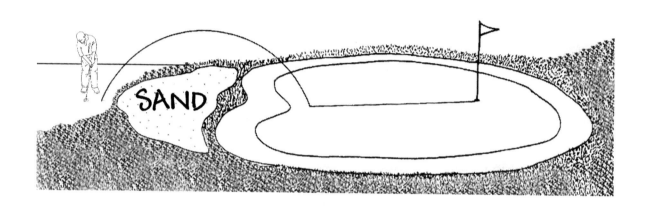

The pitching motion is used when the player chooses to play a high flying shot to the green because the low running chip shot would not be effective.

Club of choice for the shot ranges from the pitching wedge to a variety of different lofted sand wedges.

Is one club better than another? NO.

I think each individual will have to experiment with different club choices based on distance from the hole, the lie of the ball in the grass and the speed/firmness of the green.

Just like chipping you have a choice on how you play these shots and what club you use.

Your goal is still to get the ball into the hole in the least amount of strokes.

PITCHING

"The strategy"

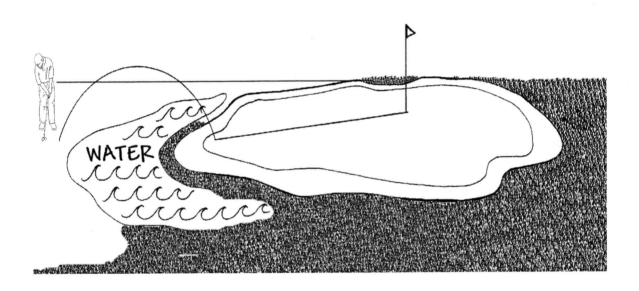

WATER

I believe the STRATEGY should be to get the ball onto the controlled surface (putting green) as soon as possible and roll the rest of the way to the hole.

Some strategies believe in flying the ball 2/3 of the way to the hole and roll 1/3.

I think that having to fly the ball the shortest distance is easier for the player because you will be doing less work.

This may require that you pitch the ball with different clubs.

Experiment to find what works best for you.

PITCHING

"The throw"

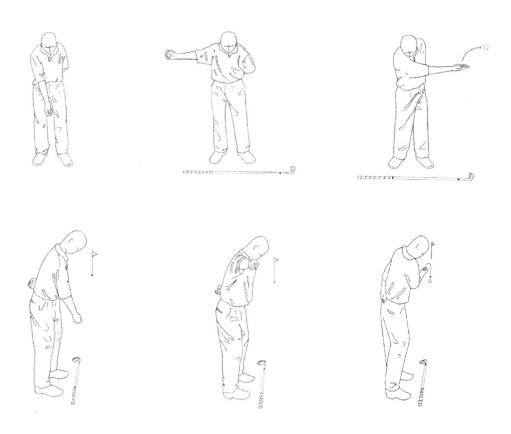

The best method I have found is what I call "the throwing of the ball" as we did in the chipping motion.

First take the ball in your right hand and align your feet/body parallel to the hole/target.

Next swing your arm back in a straight line with the target and throw the ball with your arm swinging at the target to a HIGH FINISH position with the palm of your hand facing up.

PITCHING

"The club is an extension of the arm"

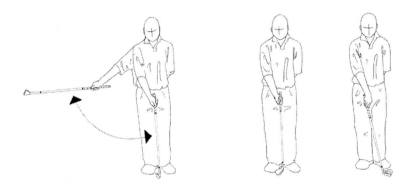

Now put the club you have chosen to pitch with in your right hand.

Here's where you will have to use your imagination.

The grip and shaft of the club become an extension of your arm.

If you swing your arm back and forward the club follows.

The clubface will now become an extension of your hand.

If you turn your hand the clubface will turn.

Just as it did with the chipping motion.

This may be redundant but if you keep reading and hearing it over and over sooner or later it will become a good habit.

A little brainwashing never hurt anybody.

PITCHING

"Set up for the shot"

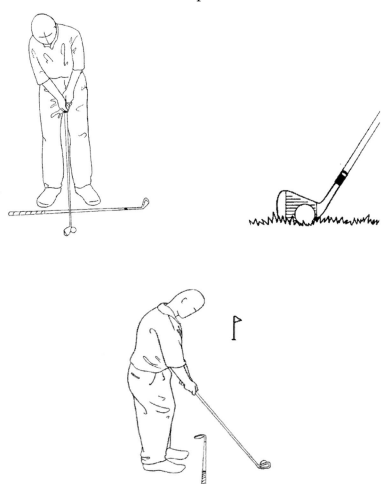

Now address the ball with your feet in a narrower stance and the ball position off the inside of the left heel to start with.

The club will be resting behind the ball and down in the grass.

You may choose after some practice and experimentation to alter the ball position.

That's OK and will be your preference.

PITCHING

"Applying the throw with the club"

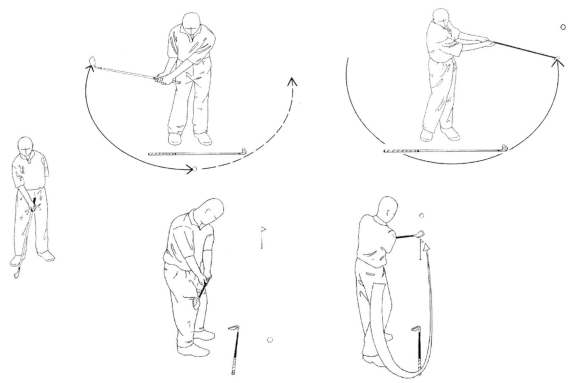

THE MOST IMPORTANT PART NOW IS TO USE YOUR RIGHT ARM AND HAND TO CONTROL THE CLUB AND YOUR left arm and hand FOR STABILITY ONLY.

Now execute the throw with the club with the ball in the way.

The club will travel in a straight line at the target and the leading edge of the clubface will also be facing the target.

Go back to the strategy page in this chapter to figure out what you want to do.

YES, I AM STILL TRYING TO SAY the SAME THING over and over again.

The best way to learn is to hear or read the same thing over and over again until it becomes a habit.

PITCHING

"What about"?

I always get asked the "what about" question. When do I not use the pitching motion and need to go to a swinging motion?

USE the pitching motion up until you feel that you could not throw your ball that far.

So for some players that may be anywhere from 20 to 50 yards.

Once you are past the "throw" distance you will use a *"half swing"*. The basket drill positions #1 & #3 will be used for the "half swing". You will have to judge the distance by "feel" with the speed of the swinging motion.

Most players think that these shots should be the easiest to get onto the green and close to the hole. THEY ARE THE HARDEST!

PITCHING

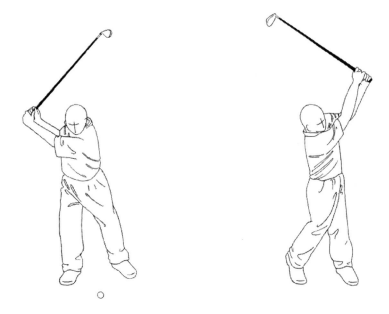

There will be a distance the "half swing" will not be enough to get to the hole and a "full swing" would be too much then you will use a *"three-quarter swing"*. This will require adding a little extra length to the swing from the "half swing".

This will fill in the gap between the "half swing" and the "full swing".

These shots are the hardest to play in the game of golf because they require a lot of FEEL or TOUCH.

Can you buy feel or touch? NO.

OR is it an acquired talent? YES.

Can this only be obtained through PRACTICE? YES.

AGAIN A PLACE TO WRITE NOTES
PITCHING

BUNKER PLAY

THE SAND IS YOUR FRIEND

THE STRATEGY
PROPER SET UP POSITION
HOW TO SWING

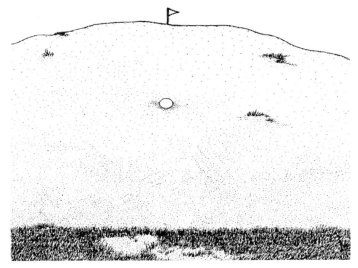

Most players are afraid of their ball going into the sand/bunker.

Most professionals and good amateur players would rather have their ball in the sand than in high rough around the green.

I feel once you learn the proper technique, practice for a while and you will actually think the sand is pretty easy to get out of.

You may think you can get the ball close or even make the shot from the sand like I believe every time I step into a sand trap.

You do not need to be a professional or good amateur to have that belief.

BUNKER PLAY

'The strategy for green side sand play'

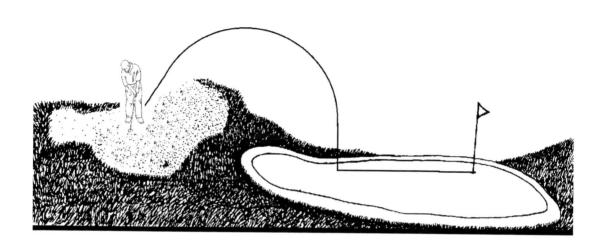

The first thing you will need is a SAND wedge. A sand wedge with the loft angle between 55 and 60 degrees.

A pitching wedge will not work very well for this because the sole (bottom of club) is flat and needs to be rounded so it will slide through the sand.

The STRATEGY for most players is to first get their ball out of the sand then worry about whether or not the ball is close to the hole.

I would agree with that strategy but I do believe that with some practice you can achieve a lot more from the sand.

My STRATEGY for the green side bunker would be the same as the strategy in the PITCHING chapter which is to fly the ball to the controlled surface (putting green) and roll the rest of the way.

BUNKER PLAY

"The set-up position"

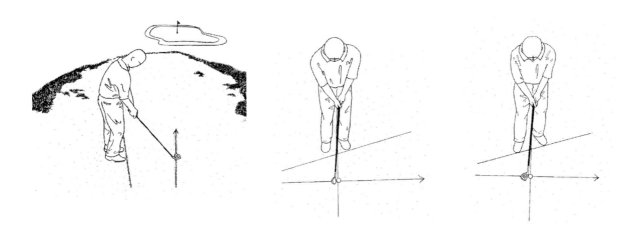

First you will create a set up position for the sand shot.

For learning purposes draw two lines in the sand.

The first will be the target line from the ball to the hole. Then draw a second line aligning left of the target line in relation to where your feet will go in your stance.

Now position your feet/body along the line aligned to the left in a normal stance width and ball position left of center.

Next take your sand wedge and address the ball with the leading edge of the clubface in a 90-degree angle with the target.

This will make your club set 'open' to your body/feet alignment. You can do this by turning your hands underneath to the right.

BUNKER PLAY

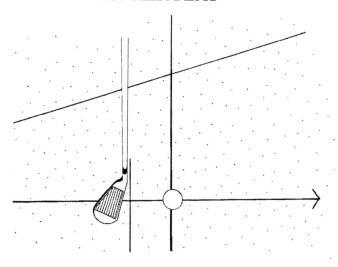

To get the ball out of the sand you must first strike the sand behind the ball. How much should I hit behind the ball? Approximately 2-3 inches. Now draw another line approximately 2 to 3 inches behind the ball.

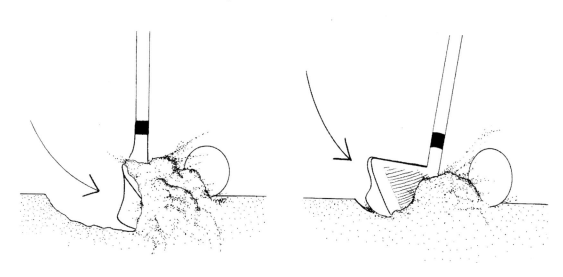

If you did not open your clubface the club would dig with the leading edge creating a lot of sand between the club and ball (left). With the clubface open the club will strike the sand with the back edge creating a thin layer of sand between the club and ball.

This will make the difference in having control of the bunker shot.

BUNKER PLAY

"The swing"

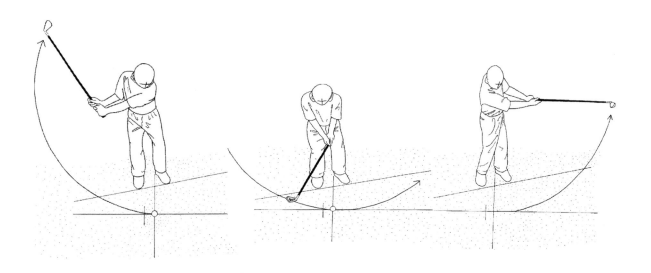

The swing motion is the same as the PITCHING shot with the right arm staying extended in length with no bending.

The swing will be going along the stance line instead of the target line.

This is because the leading edge of the club is open in relation to our stance.

The leading edge of the clubface will always be working towards the target.

What angle of attack should I use?

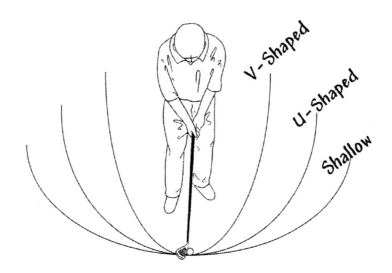

The angle of attack I believe the club works best is 'shallow'.

WHY?

Because I believe through my experience the shallow angle takes less sand and is easier to control the distance the ball flies and how it will spin or roll.

Many teachers believe that the swing works in a 'V' shape or a 'U' shape.

I found that neither worked as well as the 'shallow' angle.

My recommendation is experiment to find what works best for you.

BUNKER PLAY

"The buried lie"

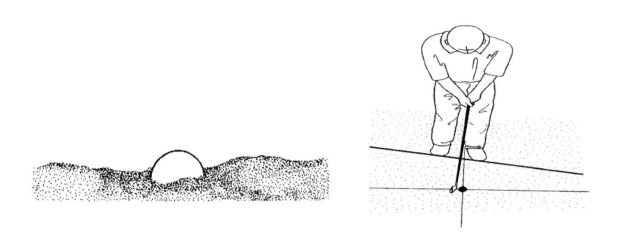

The set-up position will differ for the "buried lie" in that the leading edge of the clubface will now be very "closed" and the stance will now align to the right of the target to compensate for the closed clubface.

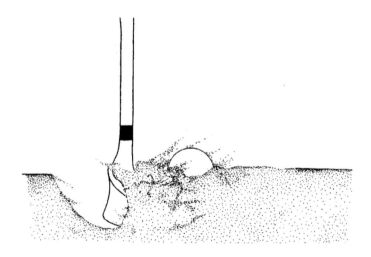

By closing the clubface the leading edge of the clubface can go into the sand much easier and will have less sand between the ball and clubface as in the normal bunker shot thus making the ball easier to control.

BUNKER PLAY

"The buried lie"

Next swing along the line of your stance and strike the sand approximately 2 to 3 inches behind the ball. You will have to swing a lot harder than a normal bunker shot because there is more resistance from the sand when the ball is buried.

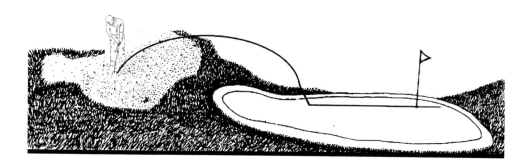

The ball will have a tendency to roll farther than a normal bunker shot once the ball lands on the grass/green.

You will have to practice this shot to figure out how much extra roll the ball will have after it hits the grass/green.

BUNKER PLAY

"Fairway sand play"

Some factors to first consider when attempting to play from a fairway sand trap.

Can I get over the height of the face of the bunker and how far am I away from the hole?

That will determine club selection and strategy whether or not you can reach the green/hole or if you must lay up or play in an opposite direction.

See the COURSE MANAGEMENT chapter for ideas.

BUNKER PLAY

"Fairway sand play"

The most important thing is to make sure you make solid contact with the ball with the clubface.

To be really successful from the fairway sand you need to have GREAT control of your "SPINE/BODY ANGLE" as discussed in the previous chapter of the SEVEN DIMENSIONS OF CONTACT.

The swing will be the same as it is for a normal shot off the turf.

Any different set up positions for the fairway sand shot will be the preference of the player.

It will always be your choice.

So if the ball is on a sidehill, uphill or downhill you will adjust the same way if the ball were on the grass.

See the TROUBLE SHOTS chapter for ideas on the different lies such as the sidehill, up or downhill.

THE SANDMAN'S or SANDWOMAN'S NOTES
BUNKER PLAY

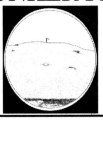

_____

_____

_____

_____

_____

_____

_____

_____

_____

_____

_____

PUTTING

THE KEY TO SCORING

THE STRATEGY
SET-UP POSITIONS
THE ROLL
DISTANCE IS MORE IMPORTANT THAN DIRECTION
READING GREENS
AFTER READING

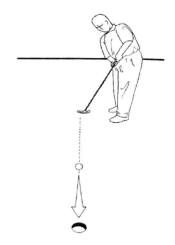

Great/good putters always putt well.

There must be a reason why.

There is.

Is it their learned skills?

PUTTING

"The strategy"

The obvious object of putting is to get the ball into the hole once you have reached the green in the least amount of strokes.

The term 'par' in golf is the number of strokes allowed upon the completion of the hole for which the hole was built.

All holes allow for 2 putts per hole for par.

That means that you will want to have 2 putts or less per hole.

This sounds so simple and easy like 'miniature golf'.

The two are as different as night and day.

PUTTING

"Set-up positions"

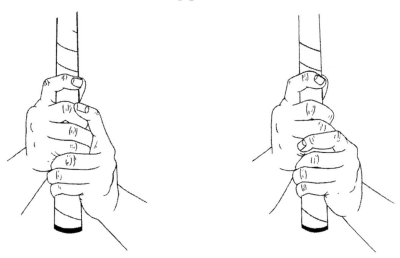

To get started you must set up to the ball with your putter.

First we will start with the grip.

The most popular grip is called 'the reverse overlap'.

Some players prefer the finger of their left hand to be in different positions as illustrated above.

I am only showing you the most popular grip and remember there are many grip choices and they are all preferences of the player.

IT is your CHOICE.

Set up positions for the stance, such as how wide or narrow are my feet?

IT will be your CHOICE. Is one better than another? NO

What about the alignments of your body and ball position?

They are all preferences of the player. IT will be your CHOICE.

Experiment to find what works best for you.

PUTTING

"Set-up positions"

The only parts that move during the putting strokes are:
I call it "the triangle".
The hands, arms and shoulders form it.
You may use any of the parts in the triangle separately, combinations of the parts and they are not rigid or stiff.

The rest of the body will remain as still as possible during the putting stroke.

Next would be to find the "sweet spot" on your putter.
All putters built have a "sweet spot" or the most solid part of the putter-head.
You will have to experiment with your putter by hitting putts to find the best place to align your ball for the most solid contact point.

PUTTING

"Creating the straight roll"

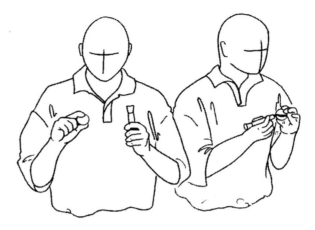

To learn how to putt a ball straight at the hole you must first know how a ball rolls in a straight line.

First take a permanent-marking pen and draw a line all the way around the ball through the logo or trademark.

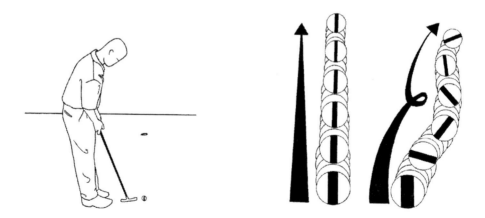

Now take your ball with the 'stripe' and aim it at the target/hole.

To make the ball roll 'straight' you must first understand how a ball 'rolls straight'.

The angle of the putter coming back into the ball will create a 'spin' on the ball.

Obviously you would want the ball to 'spin' straight and not sideways.

PUTTING

"Creating the straight roll"

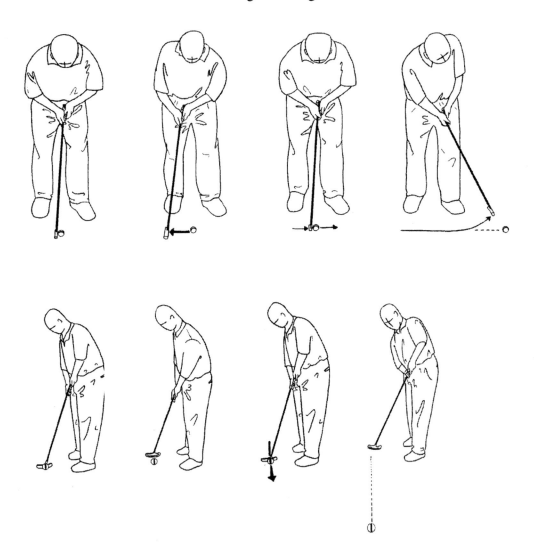

In order to create a 'straight' roll the putter must come from the low (close to the ground) and rise up to the middle or just above the center of the ball and creating an end over end 'spin' that rolls 'straight' or as some call it a slight 'topspin'.

I recommend a BALL POSITION that is forward of center to make it easier to create the spin on the ball.

PUTTING

"Creating the straight roll"

Yes, that is it! It really is not that complex.

I do not tell students how to create this because if they have ever played with a ball they instinctively know how to create this type of spin with any type or piece of equipment.

Do you need a flat surface? NO.

Could the straight roll of the ball be done with a curved surface? YES

All you need is a surface area on the piece of equipment.

TRY this with your hand and see if you can make the striped ball roll straight.

Is your hand flat or does it have a round surface?

This is the truth; I have never met a person who could not do this.

When I learned this in the late 1980's I could not believe my eyes how simple this is to do and how much I struggled with my putting before I was given this knowledge.

MY ADVICE IS THAT IF YOU DO NOT HAVE SOME MARK ON YOUR BALL TO TELL IF THE BALL IS ROLLING STRAIGHT, THEN YOU ARE WASTING YOUR TIME PRACTICING YOUR PUTTING.

BALLS GOING INTO THE HOLE ARE NOT GOOD INDICATORS OF A STRAIGHT ROLL because a ball can still go into the hole spinning sideways.

115

PUTTING

"Distance is more important than direction"

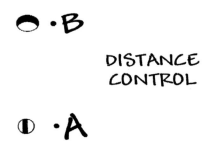

DISTANCE
CONTROL

Once you pick out the direction or target the focus needs to shift to how far do you want the ball to travel?

This is called 'distance control'.

If your goal is to have 2 putts or less per hole and you do not make the first putt, how far is the next putt you need to make?

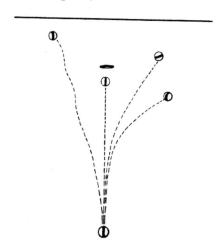

If you are spinning/rolling the ball the same way every time then your 'feel/touch' for distance control will dramatically improve.

If you are spinning/rolling the ball differently each time then your feel for distance control will be very inconsistent.

PUTTING

"The art of reading greens"

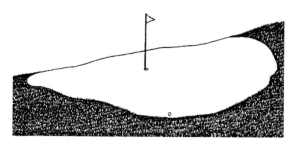

Did you ever notice that all greens are not perfectly level or flat?
So how do you tell how much slope is on the green and how will it effect your putt to the hole?

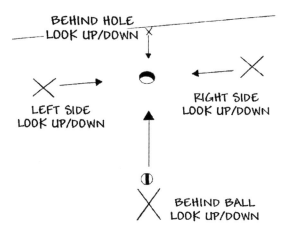

The easiest way I have found to learn how to 'read' the green is to be able to tell if you are uphill or downhill.

Now let's look at a putt and go through the FOUR steps to read the slope on the green.

First stand behind the ball and look toward the hole and try to tell if you are going uphill or downhill.

Go to the left side and look straight across to see if you are uphill or downhill.

Do the same from the other side of the hole looking back toward the ball to see if you are uphill or downhill.

Next go the right side and look straight across to see if you are uphill or downhill.

PUTTING

"The art of reading greens"

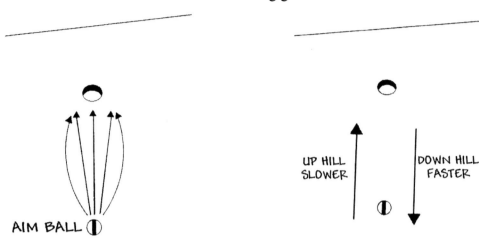

Seeing the slope from the 4 different angles will give you a clear idea where to aim your ball (to the left, straight or right)

This will also tell you whether or not the putt is slower (uphill) or faster (downhill) than a putt on a level surface.

The next part of 'reading' greens is the mystery of the grass and the understanding how it will affect your ball while putting.

The grass has what is called "grain" which means the direction in which the grass lays or grows.

PUTTING

"The art of reading greens"

The grass will usually grow towards the setting sun, water (lakes, creeks, rivers, etc.), where the water drains to and with the mowing patterns.

The easiest way to tell which way the grass is growing is by the "color".

If the color of the grass is a "DARKER" green than the grass is growing towards you.

If the color is a "LIGHTER" green/gray than the grass is growing away from you.

PUTTING

"The art of reading greens"

The 'grain' of the grass will affect your distance and directional control of the putt.

THE DISTANCE CONTROL. If you are putting into the "darker" grass the ball will be slowed down.

If you are putting into the "lighter" grass the ball will be accelerated faster.

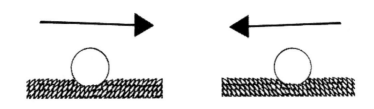

THE DIRECTIONAL CONTROL. If you are putting across the "darker" or "lighter" grass it will pull your ball in that direction only as the ball slows down to its last couple of revolutions.

This means that you may have to alter your "read" of the green after looking at the "grain".

PUTTING

"How to aim after reading the green"

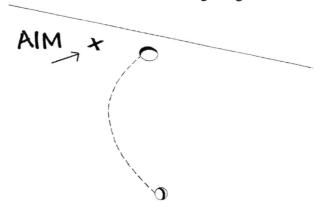

For example you have "read" the green and decided that your putt is on a small left to right slope. Now you will pick a spot left of the center of the hole and aim your ball with the "stripe" at that spot you picked.

Then you will roll your ball at the spot and the ball will curve along the slope.

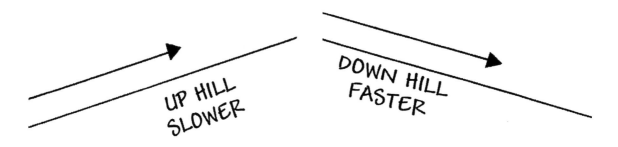

Distance Control: If your putt is on a uphill slope it will require more force than a putt on a level surface and a downhill will require less force than a level surface.

I know this sounds really obvious (uphill or downhill) but you would be surprised how many players overlook or forget this detail while putting.

I WISH ALL PLAYERS GOOD LUCK ON THE GREENS!

A GOOD PLACE TO WRITE NOTES
PUTTING

TROUBLE SHOOTING CHIPPING & PITCHING

HAVING A LITTLE TROUBLE?

HERE'S SOME HELP

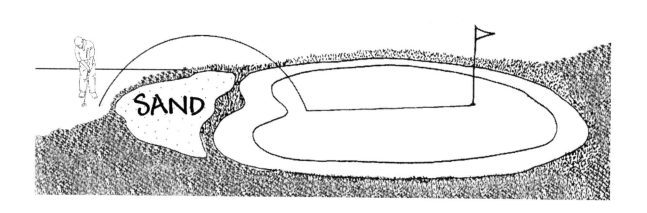

If you are having a problem with chipping and pitching shots read on.

If you are not having any problems do not LOOK at this chapter.

I mean it do not look!

TROUBLE SHOOTING

"Chipping and Pitching Problems"

Are you having problems making good contact with the ball in the chipping and pitching motions?

We will assume your spine/body angle is not moving from the original position but check that also.

The cause is the length of your right arm/hand has shortened by a BENDING motion.

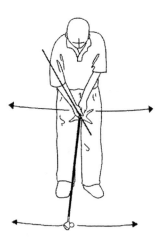

The ARM LENGTH must remain the same throughout the entire chipping and pitching motion.

TROUBLE SHOOTING

"Chipping and Pitching Problems"

Why does this happen?

I believe that somewhere in our subconscious that we do not trust the equipment to get the job done and try to help it by bending our arm/hand.

This will be the beginning player's dilemma.

And everybody else's when presented with a bad lie in the grass or on bare turf or dirt.

Just keep in mind that pitching will be harder than chipping for the beginning player because the arm must remain in the same length for a longer period of time.

Just be patient and continue to practice. It gets easier. Trust me.

TROUBLE WITH UPHILL, DOWNHILL & SIDEHILL LIES

You will have to adjust your body alignment to the level of the slope otherwise you will have trouble making contact with the ball and creating proper carry and roll for your shot.

SEE the chapter on TROUBLE SHOTS about the sidehill, up and downhill lies and you will find that the same thing applies to the short and long game.

I recommend practicing the "throwing the ball" drill.

This will help a lot.

You will find that you do not bend the wrist/hand/arm during the drill and will acquire a feel for keeping the arm length the same throughout the chipping/pitching motion with the club.

I still do the drill every time I practice the short game. Should you?

INTRODUCTION TO THE
REST OF THE GAME

BEGINNERS PLEASE READ 'MY' ETIQUETTE
SECTION BEFORE VENTURING ONTO THE GOLF
COURSE!

The following chapters of my book deal with the invisible and
intangible parts of the game of golf that can make the difference in
how CONSISTENT your game could be.

COURSE MANAGEMENT

HOW YOU CAN PLAY THE COURSE BETTER

CLUB SELECTIONS
TESTIMONY
THE LAY-UP and PITCH OUT

The object of the game is to take YOUR game to the course and shoot the best SCORE.

You will have to decide what is most important.

IS it STYLE points (how good you look) or the SCORE you shoot?

I personally would take SCORE because last time I looked they do not have a space on the scorecard for STYLE points.

NOBODY ever asked me how I hit my irons or how long my driver was going but instead it was always "WHAT DID YOU SHOOT TODAY"?

Understanding COURSE MANAGEMENT will give you the opportunities to shoot your lowest SCORES.

COURSE MANAGEMENT

"Club selections"

To be able to make a decision about what club to use you must first figure out how far you are able to hit each club in your bag.

On the driving range you can see how far your ball is traveling by judging the distance with the help of yardage markers on the range. Keep track of this on a piece of paper or in a pocket notebook.

On the course you can walk off the yardage after you hit your ball with a particular club and keep track of how far it is going. You will be able to come up with some averages.

REMEMBER: Everybody will hit the ball different distances with the same club based upon their ABILITY and SKILL level.

AVERAGE YARDAGE'S

CLUB	Advanced/PRO	Avg. Male	Avg. Female	Beginner
Driver	250+	210+	170+	120+
3-Wood	240	190-210	160-170	110-120
5-Wood	220	180-200	140-160	100-110
7-Wood		160-190	120-140	90-100
2-Iron	210-220	180-190	N/A	N/A
3-Iron	200-210	170-180	150-160	105-110
4-Iron	190-200	160-170	140-150	100-105
5-Iron	180-190	150-160	130-140	95-100
6-Iron	170-180	140-150	120-130	95-100
7-Iron	160-170	130-140	110-120	90-95
8-Iron	150-160	120-130	100-110	85-90
9-Iron	135-150	110-120	90-100	80-85
Pitching W.	95-135	70-110	50-90	50-80
Sand W.	Green-95	Green-70	Green-50	Green-50

AGAIN REMEMBER: These are only averages and everybody will be a little different.

COURSE MANAGEMENT

"Club selections"

FLIGHT TRAJECTORY

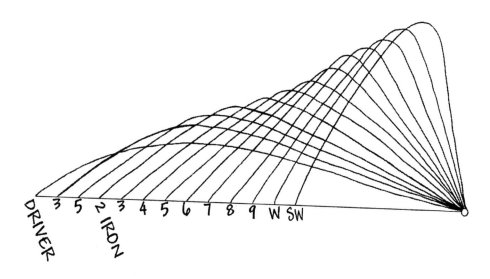

All clubs go different distances but also will fly in different trajectories.
This may have an impact if you are trying to go over things, wanting to stop your ball after it lands, going under things or trying to roll the ball after it lands.

WEATHER

Next you must realize that the weather conditions will have an effect on how far the ball will travel.

The COLDER the temperature the SHORTER the ball will fly.

The WARMER the temperature the LONGER the ball will fly.

If you play in the morning the course will play longer than in the afternoon when the temperature becomes warmer.

And if you play in the winter/fall the ball will go shorter than in the spring/summer times of the year.

COURSE MANAGEMENT

"Club selections"

IT'S WINDY

If you play in the wind it will also affect the distance the ball will travel.
When you are playing into the wind the ball obviously will go shorter than if you are playing a hole down wind.
How much will the wind affect my ball?
This will depend on how strong the wind is blowing.
You will have to experience it and figure out how far each club goes into the wind as well as downwind.

WET OR DRY TURF CONDITIONS

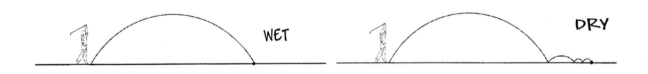

If the turf is wet or dry, it will affect the distance the ball will travel in the air and the amount of roll the ball will have when it lands.

YOU MUST CONSIDER ALL OF THESE FACTORS IN DECIDING WHAT CLUB TO USE. AT FIRST IT MAY BE OVERWHELMING BUT IT GETS EASIER THROUGH TRIAL AND ERROR.

COURSE MANAGEMENT

"Testimony"

Just for example one of my best victories as a professional came when I was hitting my driver so bad I locked it in the trunk all week. Turns out I hit every fairway that week and won the tournament because I knew I could hit a 3 wood in the fairway every time. I had confidence in the 3 wood and not the driver and was smart enough not to do something I did not feel confident in doing. AND that week I was not confident in hitting a driver in the fairway.

Does that mean never use your driver? NO!

It meant that I knew how I felt that week. Nothing was working with a particular club that week and I knew I would hit that club better again.

Would that mean I would go to the range and try to work it out? YES!

WHAT AM I SUPPOSED TO DO?

"Play your own game"

Would I hit the driver because of PEER PRESSURE? NO!

Would I hit the driver because I am supposed to hit driver on all of the par 4 and 5 holes? NO!

You must be strong and learn to play your own game despite what others might think of you.

They are not responsible for your score nor do they know how you feel that particular day.

Some days we feel better than on other days.

Most players would love to shoot bogey golf.

Have you ever really thought about what it takes to do that? Think about it.

You might realize that you could probably do that and never hit anything longer than a five iron for any shot.

COURSE MANAGEMENT

"The lay-up"

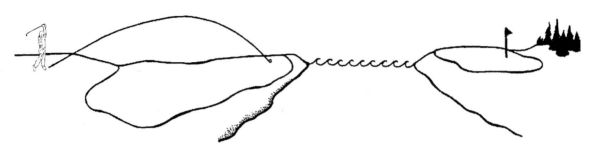

The definition of a lay-up shot is when you select a club to go a particular distance to end up short of something you would prefer your ball not get into.

A good rule to follow when playing the lay-up shot is to select a club that will not come close to the trouble. For example if the trouble is 200 yards away try to make the ball go 185 just in case it goes further than you expect.

There is nothing worse than trying to lay-up and hitting it into the trouble.

"The pitch out"

The pitch out is a version of the lay-up shot but you are taking a club to get out of trouble and not trying to do too much from a bad lie or situation.

For example if you are in heavy rough grass, 170 yards away and can see some of the ball.

Should you use a middle iron (7,6,5) to get it on the green and risk leaving it in the grass or take a pitching wedge and get the ball back into the fairway?

That is something you will have to think about.

Most professionals or better amateurs will usually lay-up or pitch out to the fairway from the bad situation then try to get the next shot close from the fairway.

They know through experience that a bad situation can turn into a double or triple bogey trying to be a hero. If you THINK about it most of us have the confidence to hit a short club into the green and maybe even close to the hole for our next shot.

A PLACE TO WRITE NOTES
COURSE MANAGEMENT

_____

_____

_____

_____

_____

_____

_____

_____

_____

_____

_____

_____

_____

TROUBLE SHOTS

SO NOT EVERY LIE ON THE COURSE IS LIKE THE 'FLAT' DRIVING RANGE

UPHILL
DOWNHILL
SIDEHILL
TREES

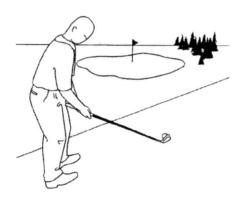

This is the hardest thing for the beginning player to adapt to when going from the range to the course.

In order to make your game more CONSISTENT you must learn to play from various lies and situations that arise during play.

Learning to play these types of shots you will be able to play harder, tree lined and hilly golf courses more CONSISTENTLY.

TROUBLE SHOTS

"Uphill and downhill slopes"

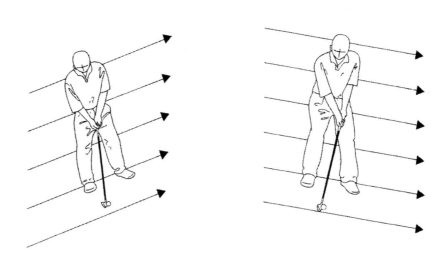

A simple idea to remember is level your body to the level of the slope.
Some teachers recommend a change in ball position but that is a personal preference of the player. You may have to experiment to find out what works best for you.

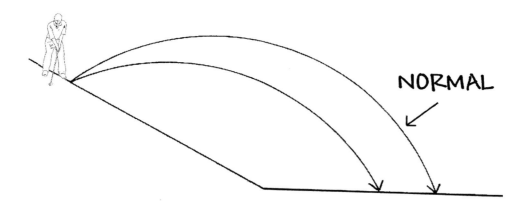

NORMAL

The ball on the downhill lie will fly in a *lower* trajectory but may travel shorter or longer depending on the club you are using (lower or higher loft) and usually roll when it hits the ground.

135

TROUBLE SHOTS

"Uphill and downhill slopes"

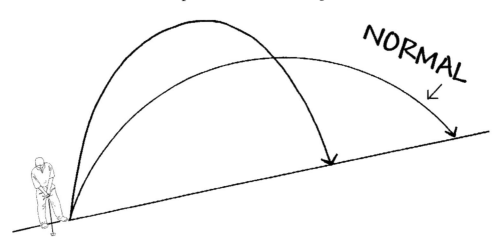

The ball on the uphill lie will fly in a *higher* trajectory, travel a shorter distance and usually not roll when it hits the ground.

Factor in this when selecting a club for your specific yardage, you may need to alter it based upon the slope.

"Sidehill lies"

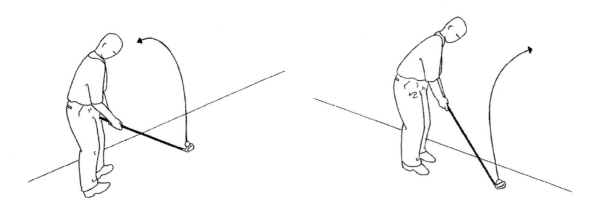

A simple idea to remember is that the ball will have a strong urge to "curve" with the slope that you are on.

If you are on a slope where the ball is above your feet the ball will curve towards you.

If the ball is below your feet the ball will curve away from you.

136

TROUBLE SHOTS

"Sidehill lies"

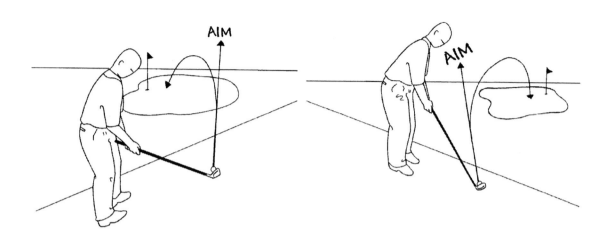

If your ball is on a sidehill slope you will need to aim left or right of your intended target to compensate for the slope.

The degree of the slope will determine how much to aim left or right.

You will have to experiment a little as to how much.

I do not recommend a change in ball position but that is your preference.

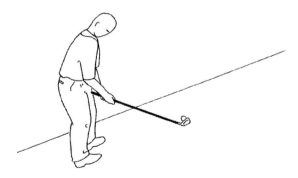

If a ball is above your feet then you will GRIP DOWN on the club and have less bend from the waist/hip.

TROUBLE SHOTS

"Sidehill lies"

If a ball is below your feet you will bend more from the waist and GRIP AS HIGH AS POSSIBLE on the club.

"The trees"

So how does a great swing like yours and mine put the ball into the trees?

I guess nobody is perfect.

TROUBLE SHOTS

"The trees"

The first thing to look at in the trees is for an alleyway to hit through towards the hole. The selection of which alleyway will become a matter of how well you think you can execute the shot.

PUNCH

1/2 SWING

For these types of shots you will need to learn a "punch" or "1/2 swing" unless you have room to make a full swing.

TROUBLE SHOTS

"The trees"

The "punch" or "1/2 swing" will give you a lower trajectory on the flight of the ball because you will finish the swing with a follow through that matches the backswing.
You will need this because the tree branches usually hang low.

Experiment with the ball positions to find what works best for you in creating the type of trajectory you want.

YOU CAN ALSO USE THIS TYPE OF SWING FOR "HARDPAN" DIRT LIES.

TROUBLE SHOTS

"The trees"

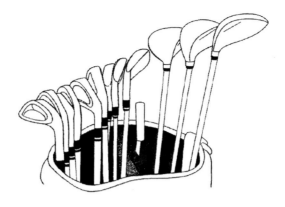

Choosing a club will be next.
Pick a club for the distance you want the ball to go.

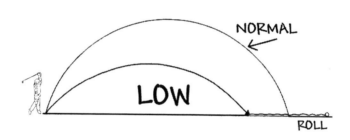

Remember since you are usually creating a lower trajectory, the ball will not fly as far but will roll when it hits the ground.

So you will need to factor that into the club selection.

LEARNING WHAT WORKS BEST FOR YOU WILL TAKE SOME *PRACTICE*. WHEN PLAYING OUT OF THE FOREST YOU WILL NEED SOME *IMAGINATION*.

AND A LITTLE LUCK!

A REAL GOOD PLACE TO WRITE NOTES
TROUBLE SHOTS

_____

_____

_____

_____

_____

_____

_____

_____

_____

_____

_____

_____

ETIQUETTE

BEGINNERS READ THIS BEFORE ENTERING ONTO THE COURSE

MY RULES FOR BETTER ENJOYMENT OF THE GAME

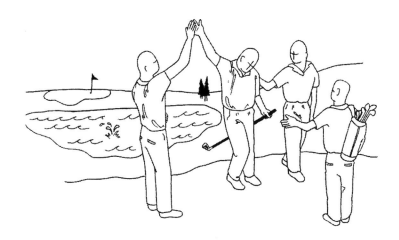

Some of the things I give beginners and other students about the etiquette of the game are a little unconventional to some people.

I do bend some of the rules for learning purposes, speed of play and enjoyment of the game.

REMEMBER:

THE GAME IS SUPPOSED TO BE FOR ENJOYMENT AND RECREATION.

ETIQUETTE

"My Rules"

After many years of teaching and playing I have taught my students to play the game a little differently in the beginning of their golfing careers.

RULE # 1

This RULE is very simple.

IF the game of golf is not FUN then please do not play.

THIS message would apply to everyone, even professionals.

If you are going to spend your free time and money on something that you do not enjoy then you are crazy.

Life is way too short!

There are a lot of other things to do in life and this game is not for everybody.

ETIQUETTE

"My rules"

RULE # 2

BUY a copy of the RULES OF GOLF and READ it.

It only costs $2.00 and will give you a better understanding of what the game is about. Carry it in your bag. I do.

It may also confuse the crap out of you.

Lawyers wrote IT. No further need to explain.

They also change it every two years.

So ask your PGA Professional to help you with the parts you do not understand or need an interpretation.

THAT'S PART OF OUR JOB.

ETIQUETTE

"My Rules"

RULE # 3

Play the game in a proper pace.

Proper time for a Par-3 course of nine holes should be 12 minutes per hole. That is 1 hour and 48 minutes.

Proper time on a regulation length course of eighteen holes should be 13 minutes per hole. That is 3 hours and 54 minutes.

WEAR A WATCH AND PAY ATTENTION.

You will enjoy the game more at these recommended times and so will everybody behind you.

THIS IS THE BIGGEST PROBLEM ON ALL GOLF COURSES.

PLEASE HELP CHANGE THIS PROBLEM.

THANK YOU.

"My Rules"

RULE # 4

In the beginning you may put the ball on a tee at any time you feel the need while playing on the course.

This obviously goes against the Rules of Golf but you must first go through a LEARNING process of making better contact with the ball.

Teeing the ball up will give you confidence that you can hit the ball.

After a while you will feel some confidence that you can now hit the ball off of the turf after your initial shot from the tee box.

This is one of the best things I have ever seen for developing a player and I used it a lot myself in my early days.

It will make the game more FUN to play and less frustrating.

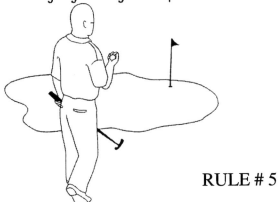

"I've had enough of this!
I'm going to the green to putt."

"My rules"

RULE # 5

The "7" swing and "10 feet" Rule.

Once you have made SEVEN strokes and you are not on the green pick up your ball and walk to the green and drop your ball TEN feet from the hole and putt.

You could even do 5 or 6 strokes instead of seven.

This will definitely enable you to play in the recommended pace of play, keep the frustration level lower and not become so fatigued.

AND HAVE MORE FUN.

GOLF really sucks when you're a beginner and have made 12 swings at the ball and you're not even near the green.

I remember my early days as a beginner.

REMEMBER: All PROFESSIONALS started this game as BEGINNERS.

ETIQUETTE

"My Rules"

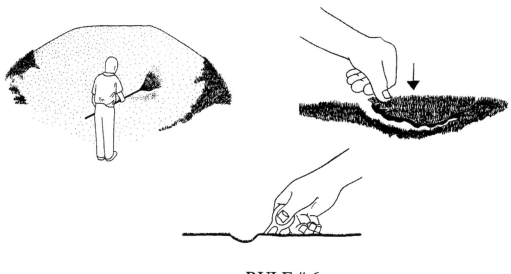

RULE # 6

A SIMPLE PHILOSOPHY

My simple philosophy is to leave the course in a condition that I would describe as better than when you arrived.

That means replacing divots, fixing ball marks on the green and raking sand traps making it look as if you were never there.

If you do not know how to do some of these things please ask your PGA Professional for help.

WE ARE GLAD TO HELP and IT'S OUR JOB.

If you apply these rules and philosophies I know you and everybody else will get more enjoyment from the game and courses we play.

A GREAT PLACE TO WRITE NOTES
ETIQUETTE

ODDS & ENDS

A VIEW OF GOLF'S STRANGE AND BIZARRE HAPPENINGS

THE LONG IRON VORTEX
THE SECRET OF LONG IRONS
THE TRUTHS OF PRACTICE
SETTING GOALS

This chapter covers the "long iron vortex". Yes there may really be such a place.

The truths about PRACTICING.

I read this somewhere in some locker room and it goes like this.

"Hard work and practice does not guarantee success but without it you have no chance."

THAT IS PRETTY STRONG ADVICE BUT TRUTHFUL.

ODDS & ENDS

"The 2, 3, 4 iron vortex"

This is the most common thing I have heard for the many years that I have been in golf: "I can't hit my long irons!" NOW we all know there is no such word as "CAN'T".

"I CAN'T HIT WITH MY
LONG IRONS!"

WELCOME TO THE LONG IRON VORTEX.

When I began to play this game I was unable to hit the 2, 3, 4 iron with any consistency and more often than not they would only go as far as my 5 iron.

To combat that problem way back then before the days of "7 and 9 woods" were popular or available, I found a 5 wood I really liked and would use it for all the shots where the yardage would call for the 2, 3, 4 iron.

I would grip down and take half, 2/3 and 3/4 swings to compensate for the right yardage.

This was much easier to do.

I did this for at least 7 years until I finally was able to be productive with the long irons.

Could I still shoot under par golf without using the long irons?

YES.

One of the funny things is that when I would give away my sets of irons after getting a new set the 2, 3 and 4 iron would look BRAND NEW.

ODDS & ENDS

"The secret of the long irons"

WHAT IS THE SECRET TO BEING ABLE TO USE THE LONG IRONS EFFECTIVELY?

SOLID
CONTACT

First would be striking the ball with the club and creating a "SOLID" contact with the center/ sweet spot of the club. GO back to the SEVEN DIMENSIONS OF CONTACT chapter.

If this does not happen then you will lose a tremendous amount of distance which would mean the club you are using would probably only travel the distance of a middle iron.

The second would be SWING SPEED.

SAME
GEAR

Without proper speed the long iron will not have the proper LIFT to get the ball up in the air and travel the desirable distance. This is aerodynamics. Just as an airplane would not lift without proper speed.

If a ball does not have the proper trajectory it will fall out of the air too early.

In order to get better speed the player must swing on plane with a wide arc, proper clubface angle, use the proper downswing sequence, tempo and some physical strength (which is why a lot of women professionals use lofted fairway woods instead of long irons).

MY SUGGESTION IS USE LOFTED FAIRWAY WOODS because they are easier to use until you feel that the long iron is your friend OR maybe you will find it is just easier to play with the lofted fairway woods.

ODDS & ENDS

"The truths of practicing"

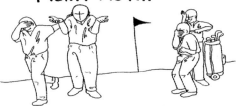

Earlier in this book I discussed BLOCK and RANDOM practice techniques.

Now I will talk about TIME.

Understand that in this game the work or practice you do TODAY will probably not show up right away but anywhere from 60 to 120 days later.

YES THIS IS THE TRUTH.

I know this sounds CRAZY. But I can only tell you from my experiences.

MY ADVICE to all who spend time practicing on their games is to be PATIENT and things will get better.

That is of course if you practice the RIGHT things.

MY OPINION is that if you want to improve your game and practice the WRONG things you will be wasting your time.

I hate to say that but it's true.

EXPECTATIONS

If you have expectations because you spend time practicing then you are setting yourself up for disappointments.

Practicing should be done because you ENJOY it and the process of seeking to improve your GAME.

ODDS & ENDS

"Setting goals"

In order to set goals you must look at a few things first.

NUMBER #1 would be how much TIME you have to practice.

NUMBER #2 would be affordability (cost of practice, green fees, lessons, etc.).

NUMBER #3 would be is this a Short-term goal? What do I want immediately?

NUMBER #4 would be is a Long-term goal? What do I want later on?

NUMBER #5 would be what am I going to sacrifice to obtain these goals?

Once you figure out these five factors you can try to set REALISTIC goals.

REMEMBER YOU CAN ACHIEVE ANYTHING YOU WANT TO.

MY RECOMMENDATION IS ALWAYS look to do everything for the LONG TERM.

This requires more PATIENCE.

MY other recommendation is to take LESSONS.

Remember all professionals and good amateur players who play this game well constantly seek the advice of their teaching professionals.

YOU WILL NOT BE ABLE TO ACHIEVE YOUR GOALS WITHOUT SOMEONE TO HELP YOU.

When the student is ready the teacher will appear.

ANOTHER NOTE PAGE TO WRITE ON
ODDS & ENDS

THE POWER OF THE MIND

MAKE YOUR BRAIN WORK FOR YOU INSTEAD OF AGAINST YOU

HOW TO USE YOUR MIND
THE PRESENT MOMENT
CONFIDENCE
SOME GOOD THINGS

The mind controls the physical body.

If you can use your mind correctly the physical body is capable of remarkable feats.

If you use your mind poorly even the greatest trained physical body can not perform.

Very few players spend any time training their minds but will spend endless amounts of time training the physical body.

THE POWER OF THE MIND

"How to use your mind"

To effectively use your mind to help you perform you must know how it works.

All sport psychologists say the same thing but in different ways.

They all say that in order to perform our best we must be in the PRESENT moment.

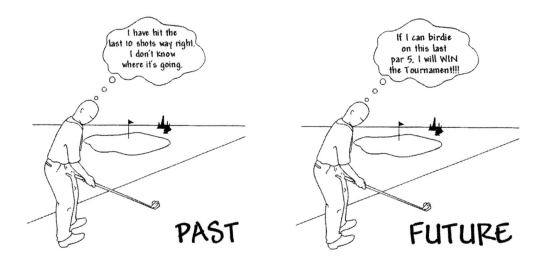

If we are in the PAST or the FUTURE our performance will not be our best and usually is our worst.

How do I get into the PRESENT moment?

POWER OF THE MIND

"The Present moment"

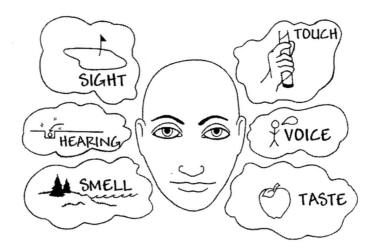

This is going to sound simple but it is much harder to do.

There are six sensors. I added one!

They are SIGHT, SMELL, TASTE, TOUCH, VOICE and HEARING.

To get into the PRESENT moment you must be in one of these sensors.

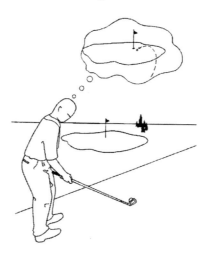

For example a lot of good players visualize their shot before they hit the ball. This would be the sensory of using SIGHT.

THE POWER OF THE MIND

"The Present moment"

"I feel my chest rotate in my backswing."

Another example is a player feels his body and movements in the swing. This would be the sensory of using TOUCH/FEEL. The most popular choice.

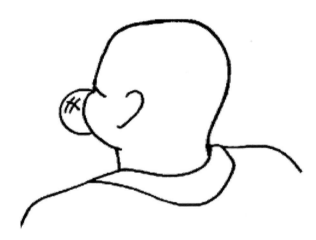

Now SMELL and TASTE might not be as obvious to use but how about breathing or chewing gum.

HEARING would be listening to music or the sound of the ball going into the cup.

POWER OF THE MIND

"The Present moment"

Yes, I have even talked while hitting the ball (VOICE) and it works very well but people look at you like you're a little strange.

My recommendation is to experiment with some of your sensors to find what works best for you to get into the PRESENT moment focus.

You may find what works for you may be different from another player.

Is that OK? YES.

SO BEING IN ONE OF THESE SENSORS WILL AVOID WHAT I CALL "THOUGHTS" WHICH PROPEL US INTO FEAR, DOUBT, INDECISION, PAST EVENTS OR THOUGHTS OF WHAT WILL HAPPEN IN THE FUTURE.

Like the thought coming into your head says, "If I par the last hole I will shoot my best round ever".

The next thing you know you've made a poor swing and lost the chance because you forgot to be in the PRESENT moment.

YOU WILL HAVE TO PRACTICE TRAINING YOUR MIND TO BE IN A PRESENT MOMENT FOCUS AND IT WILL TAKE SOME TIME TO LEARN and ADJUST.

SO HAVE SOME PATIENCE.

POWER OF THE MIND

"Confidence"

In order to have your best performance, you will have to have some "confidence".

CONFIDENCE is about the "knowing" of what you believe will happen.

We have all experienced this in other activities and sports.

If you are playing against an opponent you feel does not have the abilities that you do, you "know" you will win the match or event.

BUT HOW DO YOU KNOW?

Sometimes when you walk up to a particular putt you "know" you're going to make it before you even roll it.

BUT HOW DO YOU KNOW?

You were in a state of mind.

Could you be in that state of mind without ever hitting a shot?

YES

You can adopt the ability to play in the "know" through the practice of training your mind to be in the "know" all the time.

YOU WILL HAVE TO TRICK YOUR BODY IN THE BEGINNING INTO BEING IN A "KNOWING" STATE OF MIND.

POWER OF THE MIND

"Some good things"

Throughout my career I have heard many people say some of the greatest things that I would like to share with you.

They provoke our MINDS.

"If an athlete or team wanted to be successful a WAY could be found."

"Attitude will always win out over ability."

"The world is full of people who are happy to tell you that your DREAMS are unrealistic and that you do not have the talent to realize them."

"Focus on things that are going right."

"People by and large become what they think about themselves."

"Winners and losers are self determined but only the winners are willing to admit it."

"Replace bad memories with GOOD memories."

"Dance with the girl you brought."

"Focus on the smallest possible target."

"No matter what happens with any shot you hit, ACCEPT it."

"Behind every PGA TOUR professional is a PGA Club professional."

"Be careful what you ask for."

YOU CAN DO WHATEVER YOU SET YOUR MIND TO DO!

YOU ALWAYS HAVE A CHOICE.

DO NOT LET ANYONE TELL YOU DIFFERENTLY!

WRITE IT DOWN BEFORE IT GOES AWAY
POWER of the MIND

PHYSICAL CONDITIONING

ARE YOU IN SHAPE TO PLAY GOLF?

SOME FACTS ON TRAINING

In my opinion, as well as many other teachers, I believe in order to play good golf you must be in good physical condition.

That means you must do some sort of cardiovascular training, strength exercise, flexibility training and eating a proper diet.

Some of the players I have seen on the golf course are not in good physical condition and would improve their game as well as their health by being in better shape.

PHYSICAL CONDITIONING

"Some facts on training"

Most people think that if they lift weights their muscles will become bound or tight.

Yes, that would be true if all you did was lift weights without doing any stretching and flexibility training.

The reality is that if you did both you would become stronger and more flexible than you are currently.

This last part on strength training is this:

Try to create a BALANCE or SYMMETRY in the muscle groups.

For example if your chest is stronger than your back, the muscles will separate as the stronger pulls the weaker and creates an INJURY.

Learn to warm-up properly.

Your muscles must be WARM before do any stretching exercise or flexibility training.

That means you should do some cardiovascular training for 10 minutes to get the muscles warm first.

PHYSICAL CONDITIONING

"Some facts on training"

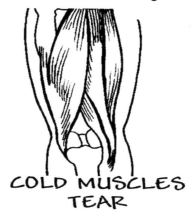

COLD MUSCLES
TEAR

Learn to do stretching for greater flexibility and range of motion.

YOU WILL BE ABLE TO HIT IT FARTHER with greater flexibility.

Remember if you stretch a cold muscle it will tear, create damage and you will lose flexibility.
This could result in an injury

One of the biggest and most important muscles in your body is the heart.

Like any other muscle you must exercise it or it will become weak.

That means some sort of walking or running type of exercise.

PHYSICAL CONDITIONING

"Some facts on training"

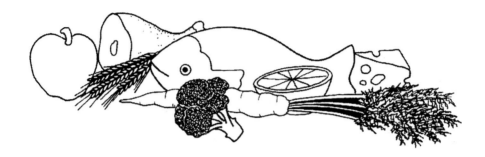

Next would be the quality and quantity of food you put into your body.

To play better golf and to be healthier what you put into your body should be very important.

I think everybody knows by now what they should be eating but it takes discipline, desire and motivation to do it.

MY ADVICE IS THIS: Consult your physican before starting any exercise program and then SEE A PERSONAL TRAINER AT A GYM/HEALTH CLUB TO PUT YOU ON A PROGRAM FOR ALL OF THE ABOVE MENTIONED.

THEY ARE THE PROFESSIONALS.

EQUIPMENT

WHAT SHOULD YOU BUY?

LOW/HIGH END
CLUB FITTING

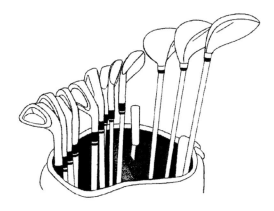

Your equipment is a very important part of how you play the game.

Playing with improperly fit equipment makes the game more difficult to play.

Do you get what you pay for in most cases?

YES

Will the high-end equipment hit the ball better than the low-end stuff?

YES, depending on your skill level.

Should everybody have the high-end equipment?

NO, it will depend on what your needs, wants or affordabilities are.

EQUIPMENT

"High-end vs. Low-end"

The first difference between the high-end and low-end is obviously the COST.

The cost is related to the materials used to make the equipment, research & development, paying professionals to use the equipment and advertising.

The second difference is the QUALITY of the materials used for the clubs.

The high-end equipment is made up of better materials such as; club-head metals, shaft components and grips.

What will be right for you will depend on your skill level, affordability and want.

My recommendation to students is this:

If you know you are going to play this game for a long time BUY the high-end stuff if you can afford it.

OR

If you are not sure about the game and how much you will play BUY the low-end equipment and if you change your mind later, then buy the high-end stuff and give your low-end clubs to someone else who is just starting to play (beginner or junior).

SOMEONE ALWAYS ASKS WHAT ABOUT MIDDLE-END EQUIPMENT?

The problem with the middle-end stuff is that there is not much to choose from and it becomes harder to tell what kind of quality you are really getting.

If you can find some middle-end stuff and are happy with the quality and the cost I would be the first to tell you to BUY it.

EQUIPMENT

"Club fitting"

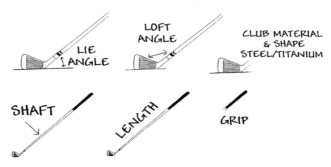

When club fitting is done properly the player will benefit greatly by having equipment that is built for their individual swing or game.

The components of club fitting are; lie angle, loft angle, shaft, club-head material/shape, grip size/material and club length.

Should everyone be fit for his or her equipment?

YES and NO

NO for beginners who have trouble making solid contact with the ball (Less than 50% good contact shots).

WHAT SHOULD I BUY IF I DO NOT MAKE GOOD CONTACT WITH THE BALL?

My RECOMMENDATION would be to purchase either high-end or low-end equipment with STANDARD lie angle; STANDARD length and regular shaft flex for your gender.

YES for all players who make solid contact with the ball. (More than 50% good contact)

WHERE SHOULD I GET THIS CLUB FITTING DONE?

Any golf shop that sells equipment where you can TEST drive it OUTSIDE, be fit by a PGA PROFESSIONAL and get more than one opinion about your specifications.

IF YOU DO NOT DO THE TESTING *OUTSIDE* YOU WILL NEVER KNOW IF THE FITTING IS CORRECT.

PHONE NUMBERS and OTHER NOTES

Order Form

Yes I want _____ copies of Take Control of Your Game at $17.95 each, plus shipping and tax (see below). Complete this form and mail check or money order to:

WOA Publications
PO Box 2448
Cupertino, Ca. 95015

Name _____

Address _____

City _____ State _____ Zip Code _____

Total amount enclosed

Price:
$17.95

Sales Tax:
Please add 8.25% for books shipped to California addresses

Shipping:
1 Book $5.00
2 -6 Books $7.00
7 - 12 Books $10.00

Take Control of Your Game is also available at: www.terrymyers.com